# Introduction

The story of the Supermarine Spitfire has been told across many years and the debate about it and its performance remains enduring. So do the tales of the Spitfire's contemporaries as friend and foe – the Hawker Hurricane and the Messerschmitt Bf 109 – yet one thing remains constant: the design of the Spitfire and the advantage it conveyed and which endured. For aviation enthusiasts, for historians, for modellers, the word 'Spitfire' conjures up many stories and affections. This aircraft really is an essential and enduring icon and has a place in the minds of men and boys alike; Spitfire also has female fans.

The famous television broadcaster Raymond Baxter flew several types of Spitfire during the Second World War, including the low-level, clipped-wing variant. Baxter remarked to the author: 'The Spitfire was marvellous, they all had differing traits but above all there was that handling, those turns and roll-rate. I never wanted to fly another type.'

Douglas Bader remarked, also to the author: 'Spitfire was supreme. Anything could dive fast, especially a one-oh-nine, but a Spitfire was quality, could outfly the Messerschmitt. Hurricane was good at fifteen thousand feet or so, above that Spitfire's thin, curved wing gave it the decisive advantage.'

In 1940 when Goering asked his Luftwaffe generals if there was anything they needed to win the battle over Britain, their famous reply was 'A squadron of Spitfires.'

There have been many books about the Spitfire and some historical regurgitation may be inevitable; however, this book attempts to provide the reader with a deeper insight into the aircraft's engineering design story, the secret science of its wing and a modern modelling perspective. Herein lies established fact and recently unveiled proof of the massive scientific advance contained in the Spitfire's design, an advance unrealized and little publicized for over seventy five years. Also here is the knowledge vital in the modelling of the Spitfire – in particular the Mk V and its variants that were the mainstay of the Second World War.

Originally envisaged as short-range, high-speed defensive fighter, Spitfire as Mk 1 and Mk II, was repurposed via the defining

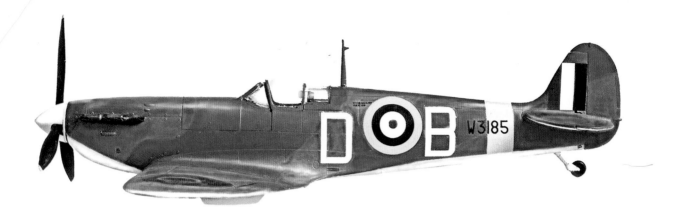

Mk V series. It was from the versatile Mk V that diverse variations of the airframe emerged – from high-altitude machine to low-level fighter bomber, floatplane, photo-reconnaissance, and more on the world's stage into the 1950s.

Just as we should not forget the men and women who flew the Spitfire, neither should we forget the men that designed the Spitfire and, those who built and maintained it. For modellers keen on interpreting all the features and nuances of the various Spitfires, it offers huge opportunity for personal expression and applied technique. Whether you are an enthusiast, a modeller, or a Spitfire fanatic of your own making, a full appreciation of the aircraft's whole story from initial sketch to final variant, must be a target to aim for. Like all books

in the *Flight Craft* series, this book offers content that touches historical, and scale, contexts. The three sections cover origins, design and use, and modelling.

After looking at the first Spitfire and early Marks, then focusing upon the quintessential Spitfire Mk V of 1941 onwards, and its ensuing derivations, we study the great array of modelling options that surround the Spitfire and its variants. So much has been written about the Spitfire that sorting the wheat from the chaff is not easy, but by referring to diverse sources and recent revelations, we can chart an accurate history. Restorers of real Spitfires may also find interesting details herein.

'Icon' and 'legend' truly are overused words, but applied to the Spitfire they are completely appropriate: the Spitfire won a famous battle, it helped win a war and changed history in doing so; lesser realized, it also advanced the art of aerodynamics and airframe design. That amazing shape of delicate elliptical planform, a boat-like hull, conjoined by a then unique wing fillet, made its mark and it continues to cast its spell of elliptical lift and Merlin power. Spitfire remains an inspiring device of engineering function allied to an elegance of airflowed sculpture, yet a machine ultimately designed as a weapon of war to kill

Seen from the context of today, the Spitfire's design may seem special but not revolutionary. This is an error and a self-limiting one at that, because in its day, the Spitfire was utterly revolutionary in its design and build; some modern observers might be too young to know or appreciate this fact. Some modern experts are unaware, or dismissive, of the Spitfire's wing technology – science that was no accident or coincidence, as some have suggested.

This book is intended to appeal both to the aviation enthusiast who wants to learn of the full genesis and development of the Spitfire, and to the dedicated modeller. The text should provide a new appreciation of the details of the Spitfire story – from its intended use to our modern affection – a tale that reaches from the 1930s, the 1940s and onwards to today, a narrative from wartime mission to modern model.

# Origin of the Species

Supermarine's Chief Designer Reginald Joseph Mitchell CBE, AMICE, FRAeS, born in Stoke-on-Trent in 1895, was not a member of Britain's elite society. His father had teaching experience, but became a printer in the industrial heartland of the nation. Young Reginald was immersed from an early age in British industrial engineering influence – in its Midlands' crucible. He built model aeroplanes as a boy and also studied early sports cars and railway locomotives.

From an engineering apprenticeship and technical courses, Mitchell's adult working base was with Supermarine in Southampton, which he joined aged 21 in 1916. By the 1930s, at a relatively young age, R. J. Mitchell's name became well known and widely respected all over the world. These events occurred because of two things: the Schneider Trophy-winning aircraft and then the Spitfire fighter that Mitchell and his men created. Perceived wisdom had it that the Spitfire stemmed solely from the Schneider racers that Mitchell and Supermarine designed. This is not the whole story because, behind the scenes, Mitchell had

a team and after 1931, among his close-knit band of brothers, there was a young, unrecognized talent who brought a major contribution to the design of the Spitfire, yet whom was never adequately credited for that role. The man's name was Beverley Shenstone (latterly a famous aero-engineer, and President of the Royal Aeronautical Society). A Canadian post-graduate aeronautical engineer from Toronto University, by 1931 he had rare wind-tunnel and German swept-wing-design experience and was also a RCAF-qualified pilot and, a German-qualified (Wasserkuppe) glider pilot. He also had factory-floor, airframe-construction experience, so was not solely the young academic theoretician that some have labelled him.

Several men were vital to the Spitfire's design as undeclared associate designer-type figures and Shenstone was but one of them: Joseph Smith, Alan Clifton, Alfred Faddy are names well known, but what of Arthur Shirvall, Geoffrey Mungo Buxton, Stuart Scott-Hall, and their rarely credited contributions?

Mitchell's men, the key contributors have not really had their reward. This is

R. J. Mitchell's design language began with the S series for the Schneider Trophy races. Seen here is the 1931 S.6.

not to undermine Mitchell in any way, the man was a genius, but he was not the lone maverick suggested by some.

R. J. Mitchell was a leader, a team player who did not work in isolation. So contrary to certain published views, the Spitfire was not the work of just one man's mind; in fact it was the work of a core team of men, most with Schneider Trophy experience. Among them, the young Beverley Shenstone brought the modified elliptical wing shape and double-aerofoil section, ultra-thin wing design to the Spitfire: after Mitchell's early death, Joe Smith was the man who guided Spitfire through to its design evolution during 1937–45.

R.J. Mitchell dreamed up and constructed this device into the world's first all-alloy, monocoque, stressed-skin monoplane, a high-speed, high-altitude fighter aircraft. In doing so he fought against convention, the fashions of the time and the inertia of a certain British attitude that left Great Britain exposed, unarmed and unready for the conflict to come. The Spitfire *was* realized, but only just in time and in part, it had to be privately backed to achieve reality – albeit with subsequent Air Ministry backing. Without Mitchell and his 'dream team' of design engineers and metalworkers, history may have had a different outcome.

How the Spitfire got to be an advanced device lies rooted in the 1920s and the first true decade of speed. Also inherent to the Spitfire's recipe were some advanced aerodynamic arts that had their roots, rather ironically, set in German research that stemmed from the outcome and effects of the First World War and the Treaty of Versailles. This was not discussed for decades. There was also a plot to get Alexander Lippisch to come to work for Vickers Supermarine in 1938, just as he had lectured on wing design at the Royal Aeronautical Society in December of that year, a few months before war was declared

So the Spitfire's tale begins with the need for speed and the Schneider Trophy series of the early 1920s and R. J. Mitchell's passion and drive for design excellence.

## Seaplanes & Speed Wings

Between 1925 and 1931, the Supermarine Aviation Works Ltd created a series of high-speed monoplane floatplanes that were designed to carry one pilot and reach a very high speed in straight and level flight above the water. The first Supermarine Schneider competitor appeared in 1919 and was designed by F. J. Hargreaves. But the need to capture speed and the need to turn and negotiate in the roll axis effectively and safely at high velocity was also paramount. So took place the change of design thinking and so entered R. J. Mitchell and his early design ideas for such a monoplane-type machine. His consequent aircraft – the 'S' series – were entered in the Schneider Trophy airframe competition that had been

set up by a wealthy French industrialist and engineer with links to car and aircraft manufacture – the Frenchman Jacques Schneider. From 1912 onwards he created a series of events designed to encourage developments in aircraft design. This was a field in which American, French and Italian designers were beginning to lead; British engineers and designers were keen to do likewise.

From 1913 average speeds for the aircraft created for the races were creeping up from 60mph/100kph to 80mph/130kph and, in 1914, the Schneider race saw a Briton flying a Sopwith biplane adaptation at an average speed of 86mph around a set circuit. After the First World War the races were restarted, with the first event being held on Britain's south coast near Supermarine's Southampton base where biplane designs like the Supermarine Sea Lion, laden with struts and wires, nevertheless achieved a speed in excess of 140mph/225kph. By 1924, the Americans had got the seaplane racing 'bug' and their competition proved to be a force that would make British designers sharpen up their skills. Smoothed-over Curtiss biplanes managed to get to 177mph/285kph and win the trophy. Enter Supermarine and Mitchell's ideas for a *monoplane* of clean, low-drag design that could beat allcomers in the Schneider Trophy. For the (delayed) 1924 race which was to be held in America in 1925, Mitchell created a curved, smooth monoplane, the S4 which was powered by a Napier Lion 12-cylinder engine with the potential of a somewhat risky 700hp/521kW 'boost' performance. Of significance, the S4 was the first Supermarine device devoid of wire bracing and struts (other than the undercarriage). S4 had a new cantilever-type wing support structure and an elliptical tailfin. It astounded its rivals with an average speed of 226mph/364kph during race trials. So was born the lineage that led to the Spitfire.

Lessons were learned when the new wing structure suffered a failure and the S4's pilot Captain Baird crashed during preliminary races; so the Americans won that year's Schneider Trophy with a lower speed in a tidied-up Curtiss R3/C biplane. The British were unable take part in the next Schneider race and came back in 1927 with a fleet of racers and the new S5 development by Mitchell as an even sleeker monoplane; this airframe won the 1927 trophy race piloted by Flight Lieutenant S. N. Webster at a speed of 281.65mph/453.17kph. Unlike S4, the S5 replaced wood with steel and alloy skinning in a semi-monocoque fuselage design. Oil and water cooling were achieved by circulating the fluids around the airframe prior to returning it to the engine. The tailfin was part of the structure and not a braced add-on. The monoplane wing was sheathed in metal and, vitally, was thinner in its aerofoil section with a 10 per cent chord ratio – which was unheard of. S5 really was futuristic and sleek. Its nose has clear hints of precursor Spitfire lines. Here was the big step in engineering advance.

Of note, another British entrant into the 1927 Schneider event was the elliptically winged Short-Bristow Crusader with a radial engine and noteworthy streamlining. Various Italian designs of Macchi, Piaggo and Pegna were also of advanced elliptical nature: Mitchell was going to have to learn quickly and act fast. Having won the race in 1927, and then again (in the now biannual event) in 1929, a new Rolls-Royce 'R' series engine was now available and it produced 1,900hp/1,416kW at a low-revving 2,870rpm. Such power would require a stronger structure to contain its torque and Mitchell produced the defining, even sleeker S6 that incorporated the new metal-monocoque techniques and aerodynamic developments that he had incorporated from the S series experiences – not least in wing and aileron design. The S6 achieved an average speed of 355mph/571kph to set a new world record and win the Schneider Trophy, piloted by a Squadron Leader A. Orlebar (a descendant, Christopher Orlebar, would later pilot Concorde).

If Britain could win the Schneider Trophy for a third time, the contest would, according to its constitution, cease and its trophy be handed to the winner in perpetuity. By 1928, Vickers (Aviation) Ltd, under the giant Vickers-Armstrongs Ltd, absorbed Supermarine yet kept it as a stand-alone brand and engineering outpost. R. J. Mitchell rode this luck and became a director before he was thirty-five years old.

In order to persist with the Schneider Trophy entries and the development of airframes and engines, a group of private backers joined together. Supermarine worked closely with Vickers and Rolls-Royce. Indeed, Rolls-Royce contributed £7,500 towards the development of the prototype Spitfire airframe, the cost of K5054 being £14,637 according to documents dated 29 February 1936.

Rolls-Royce modified much of the supercharging, fuel supply, valve actuation and cooling and breathing of its Schneider Trophy R series engine; 2,500hp/1,864kW at 3,000rpm running continuously for over 60 minutes was the target set and achieved in a high-risk strategy. Supermarine concentrated on designing-in an effective engine cooling system across the S6's airframe with double-skinned radiators layered throughout the wing structure, adding water- and oil-cooling areas into the floats and wing under-surfaces. Handling was improved by the use of trim tabs and refinements to aileron design. Many other tweaks from Supermarine and Mitchell went into what was now the S.6B in order to create the world's fastest, smoothest seaplane racer.

The third, final Schneider Trophy title was duly taken in 1931 by merit of design and by speed, although we should note that the sole other entry, the Italian machine, had to withdraw. British pilots Boothman and Stainforth flew the S6B respectively and Boothman reached 340.8mph/548.35kph. Later that year, following further Rolls-Royce engine work, an S6B touched 407mph/655kph on 29 September 1931. Mitchell and his men had created something special in aviation design.

The Supermarine Schneider Trophy design team *circa* 1930 included the aerodynamicist O. Simmonds, the engineer E. Mansbridge. Ex-Royal Navy man Alfred Faddy provided drawing office leadership. R. J. Mitchell's close associate was Major H. C. Payn, a former test pilot. Head of the Supermarine technical department was Alan Clifton. Aerodynamicist Oliver Simmonds would leave the company prior to Spitfire's genesis.

Thanks to the Schneider Trophy, the die for a single-seat monoplane with speed and streamlining was cast, by Supermarine's R. J. Mitchell. Mitchell would die of cancer in 1937, having lived to see the Spitfire

1933 Maikafer or Mayfly designed by the German DFS. This motor-glider was the world's first swept-wing, ellipsoid high-aspect-ratio airframe.

Type 224, a steam-cooled failure.

fly and, with Shenstone, having designed his last airframe – a Spitfire-influenced four-engined, deltoid, elliptically tipped bomber, of which two were constructed but destroyed in a German bombing raid.

### Streamlined Supermarine Style

Streamlining became the 1930s' motif. Trains, aeroplanes and automobiles reflected this new design trend in a radical, ellipsoid form of futurism. For some, streamlining was based in aerodynamic science, for others it became a styling statement of fashionable moment. For Mitchell it was a scientific purpose. In his autobiography, no less a rival designer than Germany's Ernst Heinkel categorically cited Mitchell's S series racers as the sculpted and smoothed machines that inspired him to try and achieve similar beauty.

Because the earlier, post-First World War Treaty of Versailles had banned Germany from designing and building advanced weapons, Germans designers created the world's most advanced gliders. This led to Germany becoming the home of aerodynamic research that was years ahead of other nations. So it was in Germany that new wings, new efficiencies were created and realized in a distinct aerodynamics culture. Swept wings and delta wings all began in 1930s' Germany. Massive steps in aircraft design stemmed from the early (pre-Nazi) 1930s' cauldron of German science. British and other experts flocked to Göttingen to see what was being designed, built and flown long before Hitler rose to power in 1933.

Inside Germany, working at Junkers and then with Alexander Lippisch's bureau, studying swept and deltoid wing types during 1929–31, was the young Beverley Shenstone, Canada's first ever Masters student in aeronautical design from the University of Toronto. After working at the Junkers factory and design office, then with Lippisch, he would leave Germany and go directly to work for R. J. Mitchell at Supermarine. By adding his knowledge (which R. J. Mitchell wrote 'might be of benefit' to Supermarine), he would influence

the defining advance that was the Spitfire's aerodynamics: Shenstone was actually recruited in Germany by Vickers-Supermarine but before that happened, preliminary steps had to be taken.

### Type 224: A Step Backwards

Mitchell's S series Schneider Trophy floatplanes had already hinted at a sleek, curved, metal-built monoplane with elliptical features. A thin-winged, curvaceous form and Rolls-Royce power were the key features. It might be expected that the obvious next step was the Spitfire, yet the initial reality was the retrograde step of the flying cart horse that was Supermarine's Type 224 as an answer to the Air Ministry's issued specification F7/30 for a high-speed single-seat, day/night fighter interceptor. It seems strange indeed that from Schneider Trophy S4-S6B and all that was learned and delivered from them, that the ungainly Type 224 should stem from the same stable.

Type 224 was an answer to a series of questions, and as such it was a costly diversion from Supermarine's path to success; however, much was learned from the intellectual cul-de-sac that was the Type 224 design. Type 224 failed in the Air Ministry's competition. It is often forgotten that as Type 224 was being considered, Supermarine was still competing in the final 1931 Schneider Trophy race with its subsequently victorious 406.99mph achievement. The workload was immense.

Mitchell's racing floatplanes had taken thin, lightweight construction and engine and cooling demands to a new level but one which was for a short-term competition flight devoid of 'dogfight' manoeuvres and instead set over timed distances of short duration. To build a fighter that was strong and reliable enough to survive repeated combat-handling and long-term power demands seems to have been the reason why Mitchell stepped away from the design language of his Schneider Trophy machines to create something stronger, bigger and heavier, avoiding wing flutter and other structural issues that had been experienced in the S series floatplanes. Smoother and unbraced by wires, yet heavy- and thick-sectioned, Type 224 seemed to be an amalgamation of the new and the old. It was a curious failure – a large, unwieldy, crank-winged thing with a fixed undercarriage and an almost pterodactyl style.

Type 224 used a highly developed Rolls-Royce Goshawk II 600hp/447kW engine and included an evaporation-cycle cooling system where water and steam were separated after outflowing from the engine's cooling jacket and circulated around the wing leading edge as a condenser system. This avoided drag-inducing radiators of the type previously seen in most airframes. So Type 224 did contain some advanced thinking, but it was heavy, had corrugated sections of skin, a fixed undercarriage in

The Type 224 'cart-horse' prototype in early 1934 with the engine running at Eastleigh.

Type 224 detail shows the thick section gull wing and the undercarriage 'trousers'.

fairings, an open cockpit and an ungainly appearance and flying behaviour.

### Revolution in Design

After Type 224's bizarre step backwards, there would come, step by daring step, the sleek alloyed projectile that was the Supermarine Type 300 Spitfire itself. R. J. Mitchell knew he had to save his reputation, ensure his company's survival and create something more than a re-invented biplane. Type 224's replacement had to be a leap ahead, not least to beat British competitors, never mind any potential foe. As such it was a development of ideas for the new Ministry specifications F5/34–F37/34 for new, fast fighter.

Britain's aviation establishment seemed to be stuck in the biplane and wire-braced dinosaur school of design and vintage aerial combat tactics. Thanks to a small cadre of men with vision, two new monoplane fighters were created and the Royal Air Force guided to a more modern mind set. Key figures included R. J. Mitchell, S. Camm, Air Chief Marshal Sir Wilfrid Freeman, Air Chief Marshal Sir Hugh Dowding, Sir Robert Vansittart, Lord Swinton, Sir Henry Pownell, Viscount Weir and a group of private backers and supporters.

The idea to develop the Type 224 into a much more advanced machine as the Spitfire was R. J. Mitchell's. He stood firm and led from the front when even Supermarine's owners, Vickers, wanted to design something simpler and cheaper – the Venom fighter design concept. So it is Mitchell we salute for persisting with the world's greatest fighter design in 1934. It was at this time that such a development was a privately funded idea within Vickers-Supermarine, as framed by the drawings of July–September 1934. An Intention to Proceed (ITP) letter for Supermarine's new fighter from the RAF's Hugh Dowding, with government funding, was received as early as 8 November 1934.

There also came the rival in the form of the redoubtable Hawker Hurricane from Sydney Camm, a machine that took old ideas to a new level. The Hurricane provided an excellent gun-platform for the fighter pilot, but it was also slower than Spitfire and less manoeuvrable, being larger and slower to react in-flight; the first 500 Hurricanes had wings skinned in fabric: Hurricane was 50mph/80kph slower than the metal-bodied Spitfire; Hawker delivered a new alloy-skinned wing for the Hurricane, but it kept its very thick Clark YH-section aerofoil that was to be both to the benefit and the disadvantage of the Hurricane. The wing was strong and stable, and in the fabric-skinned version was easy to build and repair, yet it was also of higher aerodynamic drag and offered less lift. During the Hurricane's metal re-skinning process for its wings, Hawker thought of adding Lachmann-type slots to the wing to improve its handling, but such were the tooling difficulties and likely production delays that the idea was abandoned.

The evolutionary Hurricane was built on old-fashioned biplane principles, supported by the National Physical Laboratory (NPL) who stated that less than 20 per cent wing–chord ratio did not create significant benefit. Camm and Hawker accepted this view, Mitchell at Supermarine did not.

### Chord Ratio (at wing root)

| | |
|---|---|
| Supermarine Spitfire: | 13 per cent (6 per cent at tip) |
| Hawker Hurricane: | 16 per cent |
| Messerschmitt Bf 109: | 14.8 per cent |
| P51 Mustang: | 16 per cent |

Hurricane was built with a sub-chassis, Warren girders, steel and duralumin and was fastened together – not welded – then clad with a skin of fabric and part-metal. Hurricane had a massive tailfin that seemed to come straight off a previous lineage of Hawker biplanes. It needed aerodynamic modification prior to RAF acceptance due to poor spin recovery. A ventral fin strake and extended lower rudder section added directional control. The very wide undercarriage track did however offer better ground handling than Spitfire's inward retracting narrow track undercarriage.

Today, a battle rages between supporters of the two British aircraft: Spitfire versus Hurricane. The 'glamorous' Spitfire's revolutionary aerodynamic design and monocoque build proved that, fitted with the *same* engine as the Hurricane, it was faster in top speed, climb speed, turn rate

and had more lift and less drag, all of which made it a more lethal fighting weapon, and it was an airframe that could be developed throughout the war in manner that the Hurricane could not. The Hurricane's creator, Sydney Camm later admitted that expert advice he had received to ignore thin wings and small tails had been incorrect.

The Hurricane's wing loading (*circa* 25lbf/ft$^2$ depending on type) *was* low, but it owed that to having a greater wing area than Spitfire or Bf 109. Hurricane 1 weighed 7,127lb/3,232kg; the Spitfire Mk 1 weighed 5,280lb/2,394kg (rising to 6,000lb/2,721kg-plus in later Marks). The RAF stated that a 'standard' 1939/40-production Hurricane 1 in less than pristine in-service 'working' conditioned had a top speed of only 305mph/491kph – too slow to tackle a marauding Bf 109E doing perhaps 350mph/563kph, or to keep up with a 355mph/571kph Spitfire.

Willi Messerschmitt's Bayerische Flugzeug Works' Bf 109 (that has also become incorrectly tagged – as the Me 109) was fast but it used short stubby wings of high wing loading, requiring leading-edge slats for safer slow-speed flight, and had a braced tailplane that stemmed from Messerschmitt's glider design roots. The ratio of weight-carried-to-wing (lifting) area, or the 'wing-loading', was a vital fighter-aircraft design factor, yet Bf 109 suffered from a much higher wing loading than its rivals: 32lbf/ft$^2$ rising to 35lbf/ft$^2$ in later versions. The fuselage was also festooned with scoops and drag-inducing excrescences. Latterly, Bf 109 would be given a 'clean-up' and a tall, chordwise wing fence to cure spanwise flow and wing drop.

Faced with an expertly flown Spitfire, Bf 109 often had no choice other than to dive steeply away; ultimately speed, not handling, was the Bf 109's escape; Bf 109's real weakness was in turning flight up near the stall and spin regime when even with its slats out it could 'flick'-stall and spin: the Spitfire's crucial advantage-by-design lay in out-turning the Bf 109 and stalling later. The two machines relied on different combat techniques in extremis and a Spitfire flown by a novice pilot unable to extract all the advantages from the wings *could* be beaten by a Bf 109 in expert hands.

The wing-loading of the Spitfire changed as its airframe was developed post-1941 but, it was rooted in a beneficially low figure at 22.3lbf/ft$^2$ and up to 24lbf/ft$^2$ in later Marks. So the Spitfire's lower wing-loading conveyed flying advantage and room for development. So too did the lower lift-induced drag figure from Spitfire's ellipsoid wing; the Hurricane and Bf 109 both had straight/tapered wing designs with higher lift-induced drag ($C_{Di}$). The Mk 1's crucial 'roll rate' in combat manoeuvres was a 140deg/s – highly reactive and faster than any 1940 rival. Crucially, its wing stayed 'flying' longer, delaying the stall beyond the Bf 109's stall onset.

Spitfire aerodynamicist and elliptical wing designer B. S.Shenstone at the controls of a Junkers Junior, 1930.

# Form & Function

Supermarine started work on its Type 300 in early 1934 and that summer many influences came together to create what was soon named the 'Spitfire'. Mitchell and his design team would also tour the US that summer and study new aerofoils and the National Advisory Committee for Aeronatuics (NACA) Memorandum technical data – much of which stemmed from German design advances. From NACA came the 2200/49 and 2213 series aerofoils of the Spitfire's uniquely blended-aerofoil.

Spitfire was also unique in its low frontal area, small tail, 'gull-wing' setting and the sculpted panels with underwing concave 'channels' – with much work to the shape of the aircraft's underbelly and, at the radiator mountings, allied to a smoother finish to the fuselage and wings than any competitor. Spitfire's design was its secret, notably the lift distribution behaviour of its innovative wing shape and aerofoil thinness. Novel too was the light-weight, high-strength nature of its monocoque structural design (with elliptical frames), although this would lead to initial manufacturing difficulties and make the aircraft harder to repair from combat damage.

## Elliptical Efficiency?

The Spitfire's elliptical wing had many advantages in aerodynamic terms – these principally being of lower induced drag (notably at increasing altitude) and improved lift distribution, all via elliptic loading: science lay behind the choice of wing shape.

The creator of the Spitfire wing, Beverley Shenstone stated: 'The point here is that at great altitudes where the air is thin, the angle of incidence must be increased, resulting in more induced drag. The elliptical wing then becomes important.'

The ellipse gave significant improvements in trailing-edge vortices and at the wingtips where turbulent airflow between the lower and upper surfaces of the wings was better managed by the curved point of the ellipse in comparison to the square or tapered type of wingtips. Knowledge of these elliptical advantages was first discovered in 1894 by the 'father' of British aerodynamics, Frederick Lanchester. Similarly, the 'father' of German aerodynamics, Ludwig Prandtl, lay behind further elliptical research in the finite wing theory developed by him at Göttingen – the heart of German aerodynamics research 1910–35. Zhukowski in Russia was studying such wing behaviour too. Of note, a remarkable semi-elliptical,

high-aspect ratio swept-wing motor glider, the Mayfly, also flew in Germany prior to 1936, a machine that is often forgotten. Hermann Glauert, based in Britain but having visited Göttingen, expanded such lift theories in his 1926 book *The Elements of Aerofoil and Airscrew Theory.* Shenstone used the book for his academic research and ongoing works.

Where did the advanced and forensic knowledge applied to the Spitfire come from? The answer lies with Prandtl, Zhukowski, Lanchester, Glauert and Beverley Shenstone the young engineer/aerodynamicist who found his way direct from studying advanced wing design in Germany to R. J. Mitchell's noisy top-floor office above Supermarine's factory floor in May 1931.

In the elliptical wing and in Shenstone's modifications to its theories lay the Spitfire's uniqueness, its advanced aeronautical milestone – one sometimes not even realized by today's enthusiasts and commentators. Spitfire's ellipse was not the simple ellipse used on other aircraft but a *combination* of two semi-ellipses. The front section of the wing is formed from a semi-ellipse having a small minor axis, this being conjoined at a common major point to a rearward section semi-ellipse but one having a larger minor axis. So the 'rear' of the wing behind a datum line is larger and more elliptical than the narrower, straighter front section, the rear section seeming to 'lean' forward.

By modifying the ellipse like this, an even more efficient lift distribution line along the wing, one that is consistently linear, was achieved. The wing's main spar and its loading line could be aligned with this lift distribution line, creating ideal efficiencies in terms of aerodynamic and structural implications in a stronger, safer wing. The curves of the ellipse gave more width (chord) for a given wingspan than a straight, tapered wing shape and created depth for guns and wheels even if it was a thin aerofoil.

Shenstone's role in Germany had a military intelligence link and at one stage Shenstone *was* arrested by the German authorities. The men who tutored Shenstone and arranged for him to go to Germany were Professor John Parkin and Air Marshal Ernest Stedman RCAF, both with senior national military intelligence roles. Vickers Director Air Commodore Sir John Adrian Chamier was the man who recruited Shenstone in Germany for Vickers-Supermarine and Chamier was a top 1930s British intelligence figure. As the great Rex Pierson,

A rarely seen early Spitfire prototype drawing by Shenstone.

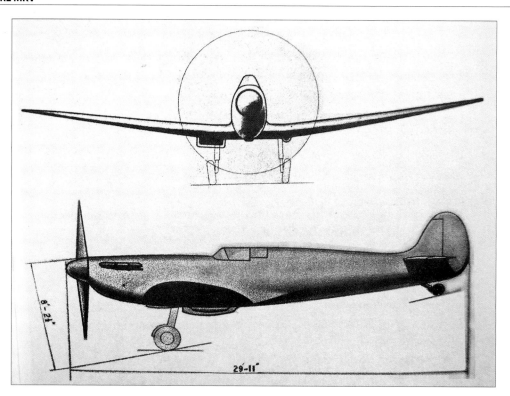

Vickers-Armstrongs chief designer stated to Shenstone in London in 1940: 'If the Germans had known what you were up to, they would have shot you.'

These are the circumstances around why the British establishment denied and obscured Shenstone's work and the use of some part-German technology in the Spitfire's wing design. After all, the plot hardly fitted with wartime and post-war national propaganda. As a tangent, the reader must be informed that R. J. Mitchell never went to Germany to meet his rival designers, yet the biopic film *First of the Few* portrayed in its propaganda that he did. In fact, the two men that Supermarine *did* send to Germany were J. Summers and B. S. Shenstone.

So Shenstone was clearly vital to the plot and the emergence of the Spitfire wing and body design as a history-changing aircraft, yet his role went denied by some for decades. A recent paper, 'The Spitfire Wing Planform: A Suggestion' written by J. A. D. Ackroyd, and published by the Royal Aeronautical Society (RAeS) *Journal,* further frames the facts of the ellipse and its influence upon the Spitfire's design.

## Spitfire's Secret Science

The Spitfire's asymmetric, twin-axis elliptical wing shape was the result of thousands of hours of calculus by Beverley Shenstone, and by the forgotten input of Professor Raymond Howland of University College Southampton. Another often ignored contribution came from leading British glider designer and pilot Geoffrey M. Buxton. A close friend of Shenstone, Buxton visited Supermarine and assisted in the wing design challenge and having written a report on airframe skin smoothness, contributed to the Spitfire's excellence in such

criteria. Supermarine S series contributor Arthur Shirvall also worked on the Spitfire's wing, skin and body sculpting. His role has also rarely been credited: Shirvall later designed the floats for the Spitfire seaplane.

Massive advances in wing shape, skinning, aerofoil blending, 'washout' wing twist, boundary layer flow, lift distribution, aileron design, and metallized sculpting defined the Spitfire's new version of the old elliptical science. Shenstone's wing was forensically tuned using logarithms and multi-disciplinary methodology applied across every square inch of its lifting surface. New elliptical dual-axis properties were applied. Through the modified ellipse, the blending of local profiles of the shape and of scaling of the conjoined aerofoil sections, a huge step in wing design was achieved; dangerous spanwise flow was tuned out, lift distribution defined, and main wing wake drag to the fuselage and tail lessened (hence the small tailplane and fin): none of this had been done before. No wonder the wing was hard to build for untrained workers who struggled with its curves and aerofoil profiles until they became practised at the art. Shenstone later said that he thought the wing could have been even thinner, but wisely Mitchell erred on the side of structural caution.

Another advance was the Spitfire's remarkable general handling at both low and high transonic speeds – all without use of wing fences, slats or stall strips, thus retaining a 'clean' wing with high lift coefficient. No other wing of the era (or latterly) flew safely at 65mph/105kph and flew safely at the transonic Mach 0.85 or 500mph/804kph-plus gateway of supersonics.

The thin wing and smooth wing-to-fuselage design can best be seen head on.

We must add that as well as adding elliptical forms to his S6, R. J. Mitchell also designed an elliptically influenced flying boat in July 1929 to Air Ministry Specification 20/28, but lacked the knowledge to define a new type of elliptical wing at that time.

Contrary to myth, the Spitfire did not 'copy' or mimic the shape of the simple, symmetrical elliptical wing seen on the Heinkel He 70. The He 70's wing was not the first such shaped wing, and itself mimicked the design of the 1925 Baumer 'Sausewind'. Neither did the He 70 appear in 1934 just as the Spitfire was being shaped as some commentators have claimed; He 70 first flew in December 1932, entered civilian Lufthansa service in 1933, and was displayed at the Paris Air Show of 1933 (where Supermarine designers first saw it).

There is much supporting evidence that the key discussions and correspondence on the use of the elliptical wing design for the Type 300 (Spitfire) took place in mid-1934, punctuated by drawings 300000/4 to /12 and Mitchell's and Vickers' meetings with the Air Ministry and the RAF's Dowding in the late summer of 1934 – months before subsequent claims of He 70 'influence' in late 1934.

Some aviation commentators have even suggested that Rolls-Royce secured an He 70 and that it was brought to Great Britain and inspected with Mitchell and Supermarine supposedly then cribbing ideas from it for the Spitfire. Again, like so many other claims, this is rubbish yet often repeated as a claimed fact.

The Spitfire prototype was designed and set 'in-the-metal' by December 1935, the wing built and finished by January 1936 and awaiting its first flight within weeks, whereas the one-off Rolls-Royce Kestrel-powered He70G was modified with its new engine and nose design at Rostock in Germany from February 1936; it did not appear in Great Britain until the end of March and received its certificate of airworthiness in April – over a month after the Spitfire's first flight of 5 March 1936. Ultimately, there was nothing in the He 70's wing design that could have offered the Spitfire anything: the He 70's elliptical wing was symmetrical of single axis design, and

of one (thicker) aerofoil section designed for use in a high-speed mail plane and transport – not a fighter! Indeed, Heinkel's unwieldy He 112 fighter that derived from the He 70 was a failure.

The only unusual factor that the He 70 boasted was its smooth all-over skin – to create a 'smoothness criteria' to give lower drag. This was achieved by the impractical method of adding hundreds of pounds/kilograms of weight in the form of 'filler' to smooth over the aircraft's skin. Shenstone always openly admitted that this smooth skin did influence him and Supermarine for the Spitfire's smoothness criteria but that he could *never* copy such a method to achieve it. Spitfire had to be naturally smooth – in the metal and its flush riveting. An experiment to see if cheaper, protruding domed or 'mushroom-headed' rivets could be used, proved that a large increase in drag and a resultant large loss in speed (25mph) resulted. Split-peas were glued in place to resemble the protruding-type rivet for the test; results proved that flush rivets should be retained.

## Wing Fillet

Beyond its modified ellipsis and sheer Rolls-Royce Merlin horsepower, the Spitfire had a special ingredient: the science of its wing design allied to an overall 'aero' package that gave the Spitfire much lower drag (of all types) in comparison to its rivals, the Hurricane and the Bf 109, which both lacked wing 'fillets' – the curved panel that filled in the join between each main wing where it joined to the fuselage. Spitfire boasted such a drag-reducing 'fillet' feature and this added greatly to the Spitfire's wing behaviour and its aerobatic performance. The renowned Sighard Hoerner, stated in his work *Fluid Dynamic Drag* that 5 per cent of the Bf 109's total drag stemmed from its wing-to-body drag and that, had it had a wing fillet and been smoother, the Messerschmitt might have been 20mph faster.

B. S. Shenstone added a wing fillet to the Spitfire's design in April 1935 as a remarkable and again, often unrealized technical advantage to the aircraft's design. Intriguingly, much of the early development work on the idea of wing fillets was carried out in Germany by A. Lippisch, and by H. Muttray prior to 1934, yet it was the Spitfire that was the first high-speed combat machine to use the device. In the 1930s, American designers embraced the wing fillet. Today, Spitfire restorers know how vital correct setting of the massive concave wing fillet panel is to the aircraft's performance: modellers must also ensure it is correctly represented.

Everything about the Spitfire was not just honed; it was new – utterly new – it pushed the then knowledge of technology and science far beyond known barriers.

The first Supermarine sketches of an advanced winged monoplane fighter were dated from late June 1934 – with the ellipse being considered as early as this time – months before the oft-cited decisions about wing shape of November/December 1934. A key figure in the summer of 1934 design developments was A. Faddy who was Mitchell's practical engineering leader. The names of Messrs A. Clifton, E. Mansbridge, H. Payn and J. Smith, were the key 1934 players in Mitchell's realization of his dream machine. Other names include those of H. Axtell, R. Fenner, W. Fear, H. Holmes, J. Jupp, J. Davis, W. Munro and H. Smith. The Air Ministry's resident engineer at Supermarine was S. Scott-Hall, another glider designer who had authored a design paper with Shenstone – the pair worked closely together.

So the combination of *all* Supermarine's efforts delivered massive aerodynamic advantage. From Schneider Trophy design lessons to Shenstone's unique knowledge, knowledge transfer coalesced in the shape and scale of the Spitfire – which did have definite overtones of boat, or flying boat styling to the sculpted form of its delicate hull and gullwing setting of the main wing.

Spitfire was the sleekest and most aerobatically manoeuvrable of the main Battle of Britain fighters. The advanced laminar-flow wing of the American P-51 Mustang would arrive nearly a decade after the Spitfire had been designed and after rapid wartime technological development. Yet Mustang had a lower achievable maximum combat Mach number than the Spitfire, at Mach 0.78 as opposed to Spitfire's Mach 0.84 – with Mach 0.94 being Spitfire's highest later achievement as more testament to its wing design. In a 1943 RAE test, Squadron Leader Martindale achieved Mach 0.90 in a test dive (over 600mph/965kph). Such a figure would not be matched by any propeller-driven aircraft nor early jet. In fact it would be 1949 before the rocket-powered Bell X-1 exceeded it and 1951 before a jet fighter did likewise.

### Turn Rate Facts

The key to the Spitfire's advantage that it was not just fast in a straight line, but that it was fast in terms of its speed as it *turned* and, that its turns, even at high speed and high g-force, were tighter and faster. Supermarine's figures stated that the Spitfire could make a measured 360° high-speed turn radius measured at 580ft/176m at 275mph/442kph (as a limiting speed) in 8 seconds. Bf 109 took 720ft/219m at 275mph/442kph in 12 seconds. Figures from the Royal Aircraft Establishment in 1941 (report BA 1640) comparing aircraft cited the Spitfire's Mk IA turn rate at 12,000ft/2657m, at 696ft/212m radius over 19 seconds in comparison to a Bf 109E at 885ft/268m in 25 seconds. For a pilot trying to achieve a 90° bank angle turn in combat at high speed – for example at 300mph/482kph, g-force was the limiting factor (as well as structural strength), and wing aerodynamic performance become critical. Again the Spitfire led in these factors.

Further proof of the Spitfire's unique aerodynamic achievement can be found in the little-known report of J. R. Vensel and W. H. Phillips, 'Stalling Characteristics of Supermarine Spitfire VA Airplane', published by NACA (Washington) in September 1942. This report really does underline the point about the Spitfire and its wing design advantage. This top secret report (latterly declassified) categorically evidenced through in-flight observations of tuft-testing on the wing, probes and photography, that the Spitfire's wing airflow at the wing root fillet was beneficial and that along the wing, airflow remained attached right down to the very low stall speed until the root flow stalled first – protecting the tips which kept 'flying'. Furthermore, the airflow at the wingtips remained smooth and attached at the stall and that the aileron airflow remained active at and *beyond* the actual stall. There was no risk of a 'flick' stall or violent wing drop; the Spitfire retained an 'unusual' amount of lateral control across all flight conditions. The report noted that these characteristics were 'especially beneficial in allowing the pilot to reach maximum lift coefficient in accelerated manoeuvers'.

The American experts were astounded by the Spitfire's wing behaviour. The ellipse had proven its point aerodynamically, not just structurally. Spitfire's smooth, low drag advantage made it a superb weapon.

### The Rivals Drag Co-efficients ($C_D$)

Spitfire Prototype: $C_D$ 0.1702 (to $C_D$ 0.18)
Spitfire Mk V: $C_D$ 0.21 (Mk XIV $C_D$ 0.22)
Hurricane Prototype: $C_D$ 0.24
Hurricane Mk 1: $C_D$ 0.23 (revised wing skin)
ME Bf 109 Prototype: $C_D$ 0.27
ME Bf 109 G/6: $C_D$ 0.310 ($C_D$ 0.35 for some variants)

(Of interest, it would be nearly a decade later that the P.51 Mustang achieved its $C_D$ 0.17.)

### Co-efficients of Lift-Induced Drag

Spitfire Mk 1A: $C_{Di}$ 0.010
Hurricane Mk 1: $C_{Di}$ 0.017
Bf 109B-E: $C_{Di}$ 0.019

## Spitfire Structure

The new airframe was made of a self-supporting alloy body – a monocoque 'hull' three-section fuselage that was welded and riveted into a stiff collection of parts that required no separate chassis. After the front engine mounting, four main supporting longerons stiffened the main fuselage section with 15 channel-section frames as hoops or U-shaped supports acting as skin reinforcers. The tail unit section was manufactured separately but made integral to the main fuselage. The fuselage's supporting beams, a main firewall and a strong wing-spar box were all tuned to a new level of efficiency. Elliptical alloy reinforcing frames reduced risks of cracking by reducing corners and stress points.

Spitfire was much lighter than the Hurricane and also 500lb/226kg lighter than the later North American Mustang fighter.

Parts of Type 224's design were however carried over in terms of the layout of oil and water cooling. Spitfire had a strong, forward wing nose-spar of D section, and a reinforced main wing spar and 21 ribs attached to both spars. The main spar had interwoven concentric 11SWG/4mm tube-like sections with five-thousandth thickness at the root easing to two tube sections at the tip – offering graded reinforcement. The change from Type 224's system to glycol cooling and new carburettor air intake locations allowed a sharp-nosed thin wing, but forced Supermarine to refine ideas for air scoops and radiators – notably under the wing and beneath the engine.

The stressed-skin wing was 14SWG/2mm thick on the leading edge and 24SWG/0.6mm on the upper wing skin. There were seven fuselage attachment points. The hydraulic landing gear, attached to the rear face of the main spar via over a pintle bearer assembly, was strong and capable of a 10ft/3m-per-sec impact, yet it was overly narrow in its track which caused taxiing issues. The pneumatically driven wing flaps offered nearly 90° of extension,

Despite criticism from the Royal Aircraft Establishment (RAE) of its very small tail, Mitchell persisted with the Spitfire's low drag tailfin design. To improve spin recovery, the tailplane was however raised 7in/17cm. Only in later years would the fin be reshaped and enlarged to cope with the effects of more engine/prop thrust torque and aerodynamics of a longer fuselage and moment arm.

## The Guns Debate

Wing designer Shenstone's notes categorically record that the idea for eight guns (not just the initial four) was in 1934 a wing design consideration and not the afterthought some historians have stated. It was as early as 19 July 1934 that the Air Ministry's Squadron Leader R. Sorley's discussion with Supermarine for more guns was first noted – long before subsequent

Spitfire prototype K5054.

claims have dated the switch to an eight-gun wing and an elliptical choice. Adding the extra guns was allowed by the chord (width) of the *existing* special elliptical wing shape. Latterly adding cannons however did create small bulges in the wing. Categorically, then, the extra guns were added *after* the ellipse was chosen and *not* the reason for its actual choice as some have written. 20mm cannons (of Hispano type) would of course replace the .303 Browning-type machine guns of BSA manufacture of earlier Spitfire Marks, but eight .303s were not ineffective. Cannons were seen on a few Mk Bs, later Spitfires operated with a mix of inboard mounted cannon and outboard machine gun; in some versions, a reversal of this configuration was tried.

Mitchell's drawing office drew up several fighter prototypes during mid-1934, but Mitchell wanted more, more speed. His S series racing experience drove him, as did young Shenstone's wing design experience from Germany's advanced wing design works, so a thin wing and the idea of blending two aerofoils together became the stepping stone to the final form and ability of the Spitfire.

## Powerplant: Rolls-Royce Merlin

The problem with high-powered piston engines was (and remains) the factor of cooling. More power means more heat and more need for cooling and more risk of engine component failure.

Spitfire MkVB paint-stripped ready for US markings

For the development of the V-12 Rolls-Royce PV12 engine that the Spitfire would use, cooling remained the issue. Clever variable intake and outflow radiator design, low-drag ducting, and large cooling area ensured that the mighty engine did not run hot. Using 100 per cent water as coolant was soon replaced with a water-ethylene glycol 38 per cent mix with its much higher (380°) boiling point. 'Meredith' effect ram-air radiators would aid the cooling of the Spitfire's Merlin.

Like the Spitfire that it would power, Rolls-Royce's engine stemmed from the developments required to win the Schneider Trophy races. Of interest, special alloys were developed for the first time as part of these racing engine applications. High-powered engines needed novel metallurgical expertise and Rolls-Royce was ahead of the world in this field. Years of engineering excellence filtered down to the 27-litre PV12 – named 'Merlin' – in late 1935. In Germany, Daimler-Benz and Junkers, would soon catch up, not least producing an inverted-Vee configuration engine that closely mimicked Rolls-Royce's own, initial inverted-Vee-type engine – prior to Rolls switching to the upright-Vee configuration. And had not Rolls sent the Germans an R-type early on?

Rolls-Royce and Supermarine worked closely together for years. Incredible power had been wrought from the 1928–31 Rolls-Royce R series engines in the Schneider machines, but the challenge lay in making an engine that would last through repeated combat demands, not the 'one-off' 60-minute needs of an air race: reliable high-torque delivery was something more. Working through its R-type, and 21-litre Kestrel engines of 490–680hp/490kW–680kW and then the 825hp /615kW Buzzard engines, Rolls-Royce developed its key ingredients – notably the 60° Vee angle, superb balance to the engine's function and consistent high power running. Engine-driven supercharging (as opposed to exhaust-driven turbocharging) was to be a Rolls-Royce hallmark.

The new V12 engine was a wet-liner twin-plug with four parallel valves per cylinder operated by one overhead camshaft per Vee-bank. It would have to be of at least 1,000hp/745kW and offer supercharged performance at higher altitudes. April 1933 was the true start date of the engine's development. Some troubles in cooling, crankshaft, reduction gear and cylinder liner issues needed solving by Rolls-Royce before its engine was deemed reliable. Strengthening, and revised internal castings were needed. It was not until January 1934 that the engine could be made to run for 100 hours (at 790hp/589kW rating) without problem. Of note, the torque of the engine was useful across a broad range and only carburation rather than injection was to become an issue (latterly resolved).

A change to the cylinder head design aided combustion and added horsepower. One hundred closed cylinder head variant engines (including a Ford-type flat-head) were produced before a production series design with separate cylinder heads was defined. Issues with cylinder block castings meant that each bank of the Vee was cast separately, which avoided failures in prolonged use. Across Merlin A, B, C, E and F series, cranks, rods, liners, castings, all were intensively honed to produce the definitive Merlin engine of production status. By its May 1935 test regime, the Merlin C was just 50hp/37kW short of its standard-rate 1,000hp/745kW design target at 2,600rpm at 11,000 feet. By December 1935, the Merlin E-type had got to a 1,045hp/779kW maximum and a successful fifty-hour running test.

First flight tested in a Hawker Hart in early 1935, then installed in the Spitfire prototype for its 5 March 1936 flight, the PV12 as 'Merlin' was further developed into 1937 with the Merlin II production engine.

Single-speed superchargers were experimented with but ultimately a two-speed, intercooled supercharger offering improved performance ($6\frac{1}{4}$lbf/in$^2$ standard boost pressure) and 1,125hp/764kW at 3,000rpm at 16,750ft was ready by late 1938 – the Merlin X. The 'Speed Spitfire' one-off airframe with modified wings gained a Merlin X of 2,160hp/1,610kW at 3,200rpm and 27lbf/in$^2$ extra boost for short duration running.

Merlin engine exposed: propeller reduction gear mounting detail.

Early MKVB (AB910) airframe registered as G-AISU in a 1949 colour scheme not dissimilar to that used on the 'Speed Spiftire'. Raced in 1949 in the Kemsley Cup by A. Wheeler. Last seen in the film, The Battle of Britain. Now restored by the Aircraft Restoration Company at Duxford.

Merlin developments and flight testing in the Rolls-Royce Hucknall-based He70 then centered on cooling and cowled radiators, as well as exhaust flows – with even an NACA-shaped duct being tried. Advanced metals, e.g. high-carbon cylinder liners and nickel-rich con rods, chrome-molybdenum crankshaft, special extrusions, cooling expertise, cylinder head combustion flow tuning, the blend of low weight with high strength, were the key Merlin features. The engine did have a reputation for leaking oil and much work was done to reduce this problem.

From 1938–45, under Rolls's leadership and Ernest Hives as Chief Experimental Engineer, there were 88 variations of the basic Merlin block and powertrain design through over 150,000 engines that were manufactured. Initially seen in the Fairey Battle, the Spitfire, Hurricane and Mustang were the Merlin's key fighter airframe applications. The supercharger was mounted at the rear of the engine and sucked through an updraft carburettor down near the sump – explaining the location of the vital air intake under the Spitfire's chin. Ultimately, in the air, the 100 octane-fed Merlin, at single-speed supercharge gave 1,600hp and at two-speed supercharge gave 2,080hp/1,51kW. With 25lbf/in² boost at 150 grade octane, Merlin could (briefly) add a speed increase of 30mph over its normal rating. In 1944, use of 150 octane fuel would, with water injection, finally deliver 2,640hp/1,968kW.

The Merlin 66 might be said to be the 'best'-tuned example. With two-stage supercharging with an enlarged shaft and refined carburettor float chambers, this was the most tractive Merlin and ideal at around 25,000ft/7,620m. Packard produced their U.S.-built version of the 266 with a different supercharger drive. Merlins were built at Derby, Crewe and Glasgow, and by the Ford factory at Trafford Park.

The Rolls-Royce Merlin II of 1938 was the baseline engine, leading to the numerous modified Merlins. Weighing in 'dry' at 1,335lb/605kg (up to 1,650lb/748kg in later engines) the basis of the legendary power plant was the 27-litre V12

supercharged 60° Vee-angle twin-camshaft engine with twelve cylinders in monoblocks, six cylinders per bank, and 'boosted' by a single or two-stage centrifugal supercharger of 6.1¼lbf/in², or the two-speed charge to higher 12lbf/in², boost. Merlin had a bore and stroke of 5.4in x 6in (137.16mm x 152.4mm), a compression ratio of 6:1 and a 7½g/34 l capacity (dry sump) oil lubrication system.

Power ratings in 1938 (all ratings cited at 15,000ft): 800hp/596kW take-off, 900hp/691kW at 2,600rpm at 12,250ft, 1,000hp/745kW with max power rating; 1,030hp/768kW at 3,000rpm. The Merlin III fitted to Spitfire Mk I developed 1,000hp/745kW; Merlin 45, 1,250h/932kWp fitted to Mk V/VI; Merlin 60 series of 1,550hp/1155kW were fitted to Mks IX, XI, XVI.

**First Flight**

Spitfire 1 registered K5054 took to the air on 5 March 1936 in the hands of Vickers test pilot J. 'Mutt' Summers. From its Southampton Eastleigh home it then went to the RAF testing station at Martlesham Heath for 151.30 hours of flight testing under Flight Lieutenant H. Edwardes-Jones. He reached 34,700ft. As with all prototypes, minor modifications were made and by late 1936, the airframe was ready for its full service, maximum-rate testing regime. Soon, fitted with a Merlin C giving 1,172hp/873kW at a mere 3,000rpm at 11,000ft/3352m, K5054 soon went up to 16,800ft/5120m and 25,000ft/7620m, where it touched 349mph/561kph and 337mph/542kph respectively in the ever-thinner air (which affected engine combustion and wing lift).

Many months of refinement would follow the first flight, but the essentials of design were correct from the start. 'Don't touch anything' was test pilot J. Summers's famed response after the first landing. Test pilots J. Quill, G. Pickering (latterly, A. Henshaw) would go on to prove the Spitfire. Mitchell's fighter flew like a falcon, wheeling and turning in the sky like no other, performing aerobatics, climbing and diving like the exquisitely shaped bird of prey it was. So advanced was the wing's aerodynamic ability that Spitfire reached high-Mach number transonic speeds of over Mach 0.85 (500mph) which was beyond even those of 1940s early jet fighters, yet it was perfectly safe at 65mph/104kph on landing. One high-altitude Photo Reconnaissance (PR19) recorded Mach 0.94 and 51,000ft/15,712m on 5 February 1952.

Originally envisaged as short range, high-speed defensive fighter, Spitfire as Mk I and Mk II, was repurposed via the

defining Mk V series. Mk I, IA and Mk II were subject in 1938/39 to a series of enhancements. New fuel mixtures, engine tweaks, new propellers, revision to the rudder balance, all added to the original airframe's performance.

One of Supermarine's problems was that Spitfire was a new design to be constructed in a new way; manufacturing tolerances were very fine and required skills sets often beyond those of the lay worker. The clever double-aerofoil blending, the D-nose leading-edge wing structure, the advanced wing skinning *had* to be got correct. Any major variables between drawing and actual product could result in a Spitfire with degraded aerodynamic abilities – so perfect was the design, so fine were the tolerances. Given that production of Spitfire parts (and assembly thereof) was farmed out across a large number of subcontractors in southern England, it would be two years before manufacturing difficulties for the first batch of 300 aircraft would be overcome, just in time for war. Late changes to canopy, tailskid-to-tailwheel, exhausts and radiators, and extra heating for the guns, to cope with the –50° temperatures at high altitude, all needed to be incorporated too.

### Mk I & Mk II – The Battle of Britain Spitfires

With 308 airframes built by July 1939, the first unit operational was No. 19 Squadron based at Duxford, Cambridgeshire (K9789 delivered 4 August 1939). The next squadron to be Mk I-borne was No. 66, also a Duxford squadron. It would be October before the first squadrons became operational. By this time the Mk IB was test flying and the early Mk II was extant, its engine and propeller improvements making a noticeable difference. Mk II with the Merlin XII entered service in August 1940. All these early-production aircraft were

The Speed Spitfire – a one-off modified elliptical wing design, as displayed in 1937.

Spitfire and Hurricane comparison. Note the differing tail sizes and wing planforms.

delivered in the quintessential 1939/40 Dark Green and Dark Earth camouflage colours. Roundels also lost their high-visibility yellow circles and white centres. Paint schemes A or B were the default camouflage choices achieved by laying pattern mats over the airframes prior to painting. This meant that there could be movement of the blanking mats – creating unique changes to camouflage patterns (now of interest to modellers).

Speed became an arbiter – as intended. The Messerschmitt Bf 109 across its early series could reach 350mph. Hawker's Hurricane could get to 290–315mph/466–506kph 'flat out' depending on height, whereas a Spitfire could get to 355mph. Rolls-Royce worked hard on fuel octane and supercharger rates to offer a 'boost' emergency combat rating for the Merlin ($12lbf/in^2$): 1,030hp/768kW at max power might be boosted to 1,440hp/1,074kW with a $16lbf/in^2$ supercharger pressure. This gave Spitfire 361mph/580kph at just under 20,000ft/6,100m (Merlin II). Mk I's rate of climb was 2,195ft/669m per minute, but a later Spitfire Merlin 66 or Seafire with a Griffon might easily top 4,000ft/1219m per minute.

The main early Mk I and Mk II developments were focused upon airscrew (propeller) design and gearing. 336mph/540kph was easily achieved in level flight, yet with alterations to the two- (and then three-) bladed props, their blades, and the engine's drivegear, the performance soon went up. At the vital combat height around 20,000ft/6,100m, Mk I and Mk II would just exceed 355mph/572kph in level flight – inching ahead of a Bf 109E. At 32,000ft/9753m, the Spitfire still exceeded 315mph/506kph in level flight. The addition of revised rudder balances, RAF production specification three-stub exhausts, revised trim tabs and hatches, experiments with Rotol constant-speed propellers, Jablo wooden composite blades, revised canopy/hood design, all contributed to defining the early Mk I and Mk II Spitfires.

Of significance, the Mk I's fixed-pitch Airscrew Company's two-bladed propeller, was to give way to variable-pitch versions (and latterly a constant-speed mechanism that 'geared' the engine's rpm and governed the propeller's pitch angle so that they remained efficient across a broader range). Yet by 1939, a two-position variable pitch propeller of three-bladed de Havilland type was specified for the Spitfire, not least to counter the lethargic take-off encountered with the fixed pitch, two-bladed propeller.

Canon-equipped Spitfire squadron line-up, ready to fight.

Spitfire Mk Vs in clouds.

These changes gained performance provided the pilot remembered to press the button and select 'fine' pitch on take-off! Altitude ceiling went up in one bound– an improvement of 3,000ft/914m in the altitude attained. Yet climb speeds were a touch slower due to the 'gearing' effect of the two-speed shaft in relation to the engine's torque delivery. A compromise of a fitting a constant-speed but variable pitch propeller was deemed to be the solution.

Good as the Mk IA was, the Mk II with the Rotol constant-speed propeller and uprated Merlin XII was a more competent war horse – many pilots deemed it their favourite because it was still light, yet powerful. Mk II was, say its pilots, lithe, aerobatic and the most nimble and responsive, light-on-the-controls Spitfire. Incorporating many post-prototype improvements to airframe and to engine, the Mk 1 and Mk II framed the early series and defined the Battle of Britain combat at high altitude over Southern England and the Channel. But there was room for improvement in terms of aileron response in high-speed flight due to flexing of the fabric covering causing control heaviness. Alloy skinning to the ailerons would prove necessary to solve the issue. Improvements to armament, fuel-feed and critically, range, were also needed.

Spitfire went into battle over the Firth of Forth on 16 October 1939 with Nos 603 and 602 squadrons of Turnhouse and Gatehouse respectively, but the combat would soon move southward.

The issue of the effectiveness of machine guns versus cannon armament soon came to the fore when the German authorities increased the armour plating carried by the Bf 109s (themselves 20mm Oerlikon cannon-equipped). Larger calibre ammunition with more airframe-destroying power

was quickly needed for the RAF fighters. A handful of Hispano cannon-equipped Spitfires became operational by late summer 1940 but wing-flex in high-speed, high-g combat, meant that localized stiffener plates had to be added to ensure that the cannons remained working.

The 'A' wing all-machine-gun-equipped-type wings were fitted to the first 750 Mk IIs and the 'B' wings with four cannon and four machine guns were fitted to the subsequent 170 airframes respectively. Mk IIs were the first Spitfires to have underwing hard points for carrying bombs. Later wing work left the Spitfire Marks with the definitive 1939–45 wing options as:

A-wing: eight .303 machine guns
B-wing: two 20mm cannons and four .303 machine guns
C-wing: four 20mm cannons or two 20mm cannons and four .303 machine guns
D-wing: special wing with leading-edge tanks for PR Spitfires
E-wing: two 20mm cannons and two .50 machine guns

Three-bladed propeller-equipped Mk IIA/B variants were operational by July 1939. Mk II was the first of the Spitfires to be produced at Castle Bromwich and came with the Merlin XII of higher 'normal' boost pressure of $12\text{lbf/in}^2$. The fitting of heavier armour plating (73lb) for the pilot negated any small increase in top speed due to increased weight. Of note, an inertia-weight device was fitted to the elevator controls which eased the heavy 'feel' of the pitch controls and allowed inexperienced pilots to make the most of the Spitfire's handling advantages deeper into tight turns and with use of 'top' rudder in the turn.

Attempts to increase the fuel range of 395 miles of the Mk I/Mk II by fitting a large, non-jettisonable external fuel tank were hindered by the aerodynamic drag such tanks created. Ultimately, jettisonable 'slipper' tanks were to become available for the extended-range requirements of the Spitfire notably across the Mk V family.

Squadrons of Spitfires from Mk I to Mk V were led into 1940/41 combat by men like Bader, Broadhurst, Curchin, Crowley-Milling, Deere, Dundas, Johnson, Kingcombe, Leigh-Mallory, MacDonell, Malan, Stanford-Tuck, Turner and Woodhall. Dowding (with Park, Douglas, and Evill) was the brilliant architect of men and machines who oversaw such names and many others and the tactics and strategies that won the day.

Good as the Spitfire was, the advances of war led to it being continually tweaked with more significant improvements to its specifications. The balancing act of maximizing the gains to the airframe but not weakening manufacturing output, was key. Airframes had to keep on coming whether they had the latest modifications or not. If squadrons had a mix of Spitfire variants, so be it.

The vital and unique wing fillet and its contours.

Spitfire's cramped cockpit confinement.

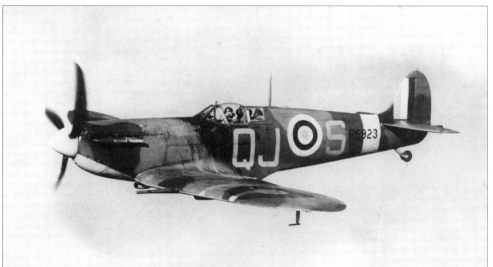

Spitfire Mk VB R6923 of 92 Squadron in flight shows off the essential ellipsoid form and hull-like airframe shape.

Spitfire Mk VB EN821 of 243 Squadron shows off the thin aerofoil and unique wing-to-fuselage blending work.

Spitfire LF Mk VA R501of the Shuttleworth Trust in flight.

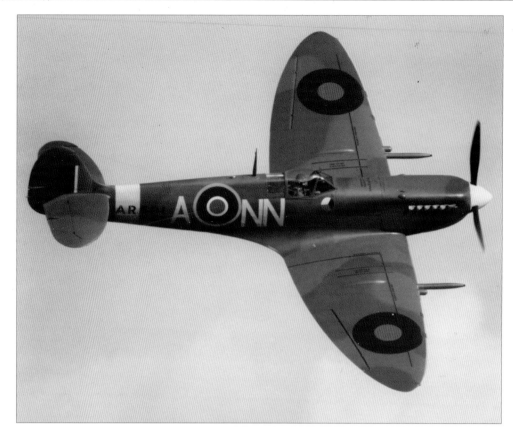

Line drawing of a Spitfire Mk II.

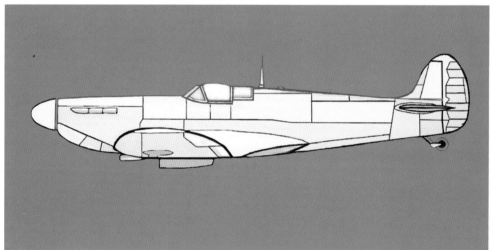

Spitfire MkV BR168 at Eastleigh in March 1942

# Mk V: The Versatile Spitfire

In modern context, we might cite the Mk V as the true 'multi-role' Spitfire. It might not quite be the lithe, pure thoroughbred that was the Mk II series, but Mk V and the variations had other abilities, and pointed towards to a bigger airframe with a larger-capacity engine and fighter-bomber ability. A mark of its versatility was the number of sub-variants it inspired, its tropical use, photographic roles and overseas sales.

A developed Spitfire with wider abilities across differing theatres of war was a must, but a revised airframe could not be created at the expense of manufacturing speed and delivery rate. Nothing could be allowed to interfere with the supply of new aircraft. With these factors in mind, Supermarine took all they knew and repurposed the Spitfire into the definitive Mk V iteration of the Spitfire legend. From launch in February 1940, by September 1943, over thirty RAF squadrons were operating Spitfire Mk V and its sub-variants.

Vitally, the Mk V benefited from the metal-covered ailerons that had been proven to assist control at high speeds. For ease of manufacture and repair, the fixed tailwheel was retained. Under Joseph Smith's leadership, nearly 95,000 man hours went into designing the Mk V series, and numerous aerodynamic, structural and engine improvements were incorporated. The carrying of two 250lb bombs on wing racks, or one 500lb bomb under the fuselage centreline became an important Mk V milestone. The 'C' wing variant offered mixed armament and could lift underwing or under fuselage bombs.

The Mk Vs would be built in over 6,000 airframes (6,787 cited), equip 100 squadrons and be sold to overseas air forces including Turkey, Yugoslavia and South Africa. Mk V airframes would be built at three principal factories: Supermarine's at Southampton, Hampshire, Nuffield's at Castle Bromwich, Birmingham and Westland's at Yeovil. Mk Vs/VIIs flew with the RAF's No. 312 Czech Squadron and Nos 315 and 317 Polish squadrons. Mk VB (F) registered BM597/G-MK VB was restored in the 1990s by the Historic Aircraft Collection at Duxford as one of the seven restored Mk V series of the modern age.

February 1941 saw the introduction of the first Mk V. The Battle of Britain had

Spitfire Mk Vs of 611 Squadron.

reached its height in the closing days of the summer of 1940, yet a battle still raged in the skies and night-fighter operations were also established. The North Africa campaign, Malta's plight, Pacific theatre demands and ultimately low-level strikes in Europe were to be key Mk V themes.

Soon the RAF would go from the defensive combat of Britain and begin sending Spitfires into German-occupied French airspace. The war would also take to the air at low level, in the tropics and in the desert. Mk V would see service as far afield as Australia, Burma, Egypt and Africa. By sacrificing a bit of the original Spitfire's lighter controls and handling, a much more versatile, more powerful, better-armed airframe could be created. Cannons, bomb racks, larger radiators, tuned power for differing combat altitudes, all manifested in the Mk V and its derivatives. A few earlier 1940-built Mk Is were converted to 'interim' Mk V specification, including airframe R6923. One Mk V two-seater trainer was constructed in South African service with No. 4 Squadron SAAF in 1943.

The Germans had also developed the Bf 109 and were soon to debut the Focke-Wulf 190 – another fast but underwinged airframe but which could outpace an early Spitfire – especially one that lacked modifications to its fuel feed for inverted flight. But Fw190 had wing loading of 39lbf/ft$^2$ which was around 15lbf/ft$^2$ *more* than a Spitfire and therefore could be decisively out-turned by the British machine. But the Fw190 was fast in normal flight, faster than the Mk V.

The Mk V entered British service with No. 92 Squadron in February 1941 and then No. 91 in March and Nos 54 and 603 squadrons in April. From May, Nos 74, 111, 609 and 611 squadrons became Mk V-equipped. Across the summer and into the autumn of that year, Nos 72, 303, 616, 450 and 40 squadrons received their machines. Nos 350 and 402 squadrons had to wait until February/March 1942.

Of note, prior to Mk V, the Mk III was a limited configuration non-production series variant first flown in March 1940 as a Mk I conversion with modified clipped wings, retractable tailwheel and Merlin XX. It was later reconfigured with standard wingtips. Next, the Mk IV also did not come to fruition because the revised engine intended for it was not ready – the idea would manifest in the later Griffon-engined Spitfire variants. The 36.7 litre 1,450hp Griffon was longer and heavier. So Spitfire went from Mk II to Mk V. Latterly, as the Mk V generic series were developed, the Mk III prototype then lent its features to the Mk VB which then framed the Mks VII, VIII, and F21/22 and the very different airframes of Mk IX and Mk XIV.

The early Mk VA model soon replaced Mk I and Mk IIs at squadron level, but latter Mk V series (a 1,000 airframe order) came in a delivery schedule that was non-linear – the VA debuted in 1941 and then the new-build VB series gained in numbers with further variants that used the VB's improved joint, cannon/machine gun-equipped wing design.

As early as April 1941, a Mk V was fitted with an experimental four-bladed propeller and achieved major gains in climb speed (four minutes faster to 39,000ft), yet only 10mph quicker at optimum cruise height. A range of 'Universal C' wings, and propeller variations were tried out on Mk Vs in various locations across the world – sometimes dictated by spare parts availability or the lack thereof.

More power (1,470hp) came from the revised Merlin 45 which gained more power at higher altitude via a revised air-intake system. Merlin's Mk 45, 46, and 50(A) were fitted to the Mk Vs longer nose. The engine bearer-longerons had to be strengthened in order to take the small increase in the revised Merlin's weight, demonstrating just how fine the Spitfire's engineering tolerances were. Merlin M series engines (45M, 50M, 55M) with negative-G carburettors and fuel de-aerators tuned to lower-altitude combustion and torque efficiency demonstrated just how well the Mk V could be specified.

Mk V in its A-variant used the wings from the Spitfire Mk IIA, whereas the Mk VB used the wings of the Mk IIB. Mk VC used the modified, universal wing – principally with mixed armament. Extra ammunition rounds could be accommodated in the

Spitfire LFMkVC, AR501 cockpit detail.

Returning from combat. Bomb racks empty. This late model, canon-equipped variant looks well used but the Merlin is still singing somewhere in the Mediterranean theatre of war during service with 126 Squadron or perhaps 1435 Unit/Squadron.

Spitfire Mk VB (Trop) arrestor hook modifications to BL687.

revised wing. All Mk Vs had better armour plating near the fuel tanks, ammunition boxes and for the pilot's seat. High-altitude combat required extra heating for the armament to stop it freezing – extra piping took engine exhaust-bled hot air to the outer wings.

In Mk I form the Spitfire had a weight (loaded) 5,280lb on RAF service entry. Under three years later, in Mk V form, Spitfire had got to a loaded weight of 6,417lb, but it could now get to 1mph shy of 370mph in level flight. Maximum diving speed exceeded 500mph.

Certain, later-model Mk VB and VC airframes used the squared-off clipped wings of 30ft 6in/9.3m span for low-level combat use. Removing the elliptical tip reduced the aircraft's turning ability at high altitudes, increased drag and reduced top speed, but it did increase the roll-rate at very low altitude for ground-attack roles and mid-range climb speed was improved too; fitment of a tuned Merlin 46 giving better power at 15,000ft added to capability.

Tropical variant Mk Vs and later Marks (some built at Vickers' South Marston factory) used a reduced power Merlin 45–55 series with cropped supercharger blades. Designated the 45M, 50M and 55M, this measure reduced ultimate boost but gave better full-throttle 'charge' response at different altitudes to the normal supercharger effect. Tropical Spitfires with larger air intakes saw Mk VC use the 'Vokes' Aero Vee tropical filter in a distinctive larger undernose fairing. An underbelly 'Aboukir' type intake was developed by No. 103 Maintenance Unit in Egypt. The tropicalized Mk VC offered an external 30-gallon belly-mounted faired-in slipper tank giving a 690-mile range.

There could also be wire mesh guards over intakes: such features might slow a Spitfire by up to 10mph, showing just how finite the design and the smooth skin had been; minor disturbances had major effects (Arctic-use Spitfires also needed mesh guards over the main intake).

Keeping up with developed Bf 109F series was vital in 1941 and the German machine could reach 385mph and equal the Spitfire's ceiling. But Mk V retained its climb and turn-rate advantage.

Mk VA (Trop) with long-range underbelly tank and revised exhausts.

This Mk VB displays hard-use and 'weathering' and proves just what level of distress a front-line airframe suffered.

American Eagles. Crews scramble under the stars and stripes to their Mk Vs.

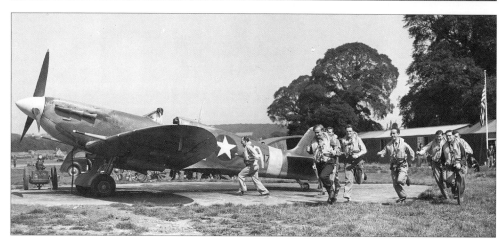

An extra electric fuel pump was fitted due to temperature effects on the fuel supply. Later models of the Mk V, notably tropical variants, used a fuel system that saw what was effectively air-pressure feed from the vacuum pump venting into the top tank.

### Floatplane

Type 355 Mk VB floatplane conversions to Mk VB (W3760) and one to Mk IX standards included extra finlets and water rudders latterly added. After early one-off experiments in 1940 with existing Blackburn Company floats on a Mk I, totally new floats were designed by Supermarine, built by Folland Ltd and fitted to the Mk VB for testing. Twelve sets of floats (for six airframes) were constructed. Numerous tail surface, exhaust, air intake and airscrew variations were tried. Main spars were reinforced to accept main float attachment lugs. Take-off speed: 83mph; landing speed: 100mph; loaded weight: 7,508lb. Despite the very long Supermarine floats (25.59ft) in-flight handling remained excellent and the vital turn, stall and spin behaviours were only marginally degraded. The taller fin and rudder above and below the fuselage datum line restored directional stability. Lead Mk V floatplane airframes were W3570, EP751 and EP754. A Mk IX-based floatplane was MJ892 July 1944. A Mk21 Griffon-engined floatplane was also considered Overtaken by events, there was no series production of Spitfire floatplanes but there were highly successful testing results, with the idea of Pacific and Mediterranean deployment. Mk V also saw Soviet Red Air Force service from

Mk VBs of the 31st Fighter Group USAAF in North Africa, 1943.

## Spitfire Type 349 Mk V series and sub-variants principal modifications

Strengthened fuselage with skin plating increased up to 24 SWG to rear fuselage boom

B- or C-type wings

Fitting of bomb racks to wings

Optional changes to wingtip shape

Metal-skinned ailerons

Thicker alloy skin (3mm) over top fuel tank 3mm thick

Engine upgrades with revised Merlins

Longer propeller spinner and Rotol-type blades

Exhaust ejector changes, 'fishtail' shapes with gun heating tubes, flame-damping slits

Piping from rear pipe of exhaust stack to heat gun bays

Longer engine bay/nose with Merlin 60 series to sub-variants

Carburettor feed improvements (diaphragm type after early orifice restrictors in Merlin 50 series)

2 x, 4 x cannon and machine gun armament choices (one aircraft W3237 fitted with 8 x cannon).

Increased cannon and bullet capacity in armour boxes

Extra wing heating to armament

Hood and canopy changes (including Malcolm Ltd hood) and Mk VII sliding canopy

External windscreen armour to VA/B canopy

Interior armoured glass windscreen from VC series and some earlier variants

Jettisonable canopy

Modified voltage regulator in cockpit behind pilot's headrest

Modifications to radio mast/aerial.

2-inch forward extension to undercarriage legs to VC series

Optional 170-gallon external fuel tank giving 284 gallons and max still-air range of 1,625 miles.

Optional 30-, 45-, 90-gallon fuel drop-tanks. Possible 29-gallon rear fuselage tank

Optional electrically charged glider tow rope release

1942, notably with a rearwards-facing loop aerial. Mk VIs were Russian-operated from 1942 having been handed over for Arctic convoy duties. Mk V was also a glider tow tug. Two and even three Mk Vs towing a linked cable could tow a laden Horsa- or Hotspur-type glider over hundreds of miles – weather dependent.

By 1943, the baseline Mk V had been superseded in Europe, but its sub-variants and the resultant Marks owe it much.

### American Wings

The Americans got their hands on a Spitfire as early as September 1939, when a very early Mk I airframe, L1090, was shipped to the USAAC flight test facility at Wright Field, Ohio. After extensive evaluation, the airframe was then flown to Canada in May 1940 for RCAF testing. The aircraft returned to Great Britain in the summer of that year. One Mk V and later in 1943, a Seafire IIC were also transported to the United States for testing.

For the Americans, well served with their own rush of fighter types, the use of the Spitfire was intended as 'stop-gap' temporary measure, but it was one that lasted until late 1945: the P-39 Aircobra as a fighter interceptor in USAAC/ USAAF and RAF service was not a success. Spitfire Mk Vs were soon substituted. Approximately 1,000 Spitfires found their way into American hands. The American experts had realized that the Spitfire 'turned on a dime' and was highly manoeuvrable. An attempt to re-equip the USAAF in 1943 with the elliptically winged P-47 Thunderbolt (to replace Spitfires) caused problems when transferring pilots found that the P-47 would spin dangerously in a turn that would not have troubled a Spitfire. Several P-47 pilots were killed.

The American 'Eagle' squadrons (Nos 71, 121, 131) received Spitfire Mk VB airframes from November/December 1941. By September 1942 the Eagle groups' Mk Vs were in Debden-based USAAF 4th Fighter Group markings flying as the 334th, 335th and 336th fighter squadrons; Mk VCs were operated into 1943.

Other American USAAF fighter units that used the Mk V series included 6th Fighter Wing (FW) training unit, 14th Fighter Group (FG) training unit, 66th FW combat unit from Duxford, 81st FG Combat unit using Mk VBs from Atcham, the 308th FS at Kenley, the 350th FG Combat unit at Duxford, 495th and 496th FTGs as combat and training units respectively from Atcham, Goxhill and Halesworth 1943–45. The 31st Fighter Group did not receive its P-39 Aircobras on time and became a Mk V operator. Based at Westhampnett, this unit became the first group of the Eighth Air Force to become operational. Lieutenant-Colonel Don Blakeslee with 15 kills was the leader who achieved greatness on American Spitfire wings. Lieutenant Don Gentile, an original RAF Eagle Squadron member, was the top American ace with 21 kills. The Tactical Reconnaissance Group operating Mk VIs was based at Membury, as was the 1st Fighter Group of the mighty Eighth Air Force.

Early 31st and 52nd Group deployments were as defensive sweeps and as escorts to bombers. The Dieppe raids provided the groups with combat experience prior to being part of Operation Torch in North Africa. The Eighth Air Force moved to North Africa to join the Twelfth Air Force operating Mk VC (Trop) machines, initially based from Tafaraoui in Algeria in November 1942. By July 1943, these USAAF Spitfires were sweeping over Italian skies as the Allies moved northward through Italy. P-51B Mustangs would take over and the last 31st Fighter Group Mk V sorties in Italy took place around 28/29 March 1943.

The 52nd Fighter Group, initially based in Northern Ireland and then in Lincolnshire, operated from July 1942 to March 1944. This included deployment to Gibraltar, North Africa and Italy.

Mk Vs and X1s were also operated by the Photo-Reconnaissance Groups (PG) of the 7th, 10th and 67th PGs through the 12th, 14th and 15th squadrons. These photo-recce groups were mainly based in Berkshire and Oxfordshire, where Major W. Weitner commanded the 14th unit: his was the first US-operated PR Spitfire to fly over Berlin. After D-Day they moved to France (Brittany) and then into Germany in 1945. During the Operation Overlord landings, USAAF Spitfire pilots operated, some of them in British in markings but notably under US Navy control as part of the 'Air Spotting Pool' for less than sixty days. Little known were the US Navy-marked Mk VBs briefly operated from Lee-on-Solent in June 1944 under 'VCS-7' (see model photos). Also little known was the use of a Mk VB by Brigadier General James Doolittle in North Africa in 1943; Doolittle had won the 1925 Schneider Trophy race!

By early 1942, over 1,500 Mk V Series had been delivered: Mk Vs entered service in the Mediterranean theatre at Malta in April 1942. Mk Vs entered the Middle East with No. 145 Squadron in June 1942. The RAF's Western Desert squadrons Nos 145 and 92 received their Mk Vs in April/May. Nos 601 and 417 squadrons were Mk V-equipped by October 1942 and by January 1943 No. 54 Squadron located at Darwin, Northern Territory Australia was given Mk Vs as the first unit to operate Spitfires in the Pacific arena. The Japanese threat to Australia saw British Spitfire squadrons Nos 452 and 457 relocated to Australia's defence force. Mk VIIIs also found their way to the Northern Territory.

Mk VB as BR372 was experimentally fitted with split, trailing-edge speed-brakes. One pressurized Mk VB flew at an indicated 49,790ft in 1942. Spitfire Mk VB EN830 was captured by the Luftwaffe and re-engined with the rival Bf 109's Daimler-Benz 605A engine of 1,450hp. Flown at a weight of approximately 6,000lb, its combat-weary airframe achieved 379.8mph at 22,000ft.

Thanks to MK V, Spitfire would have many guises.

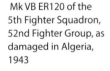

Mk VB ER120 of the 5th Fighter Squadron, 52nd Fighter Group, as damaged in Algeria, 1943

Mk VC at Ponte Olivio during American operations in 1943. Note Vokes filter and bubble canopy.

Mk VB paint-stripped ready for US markings to be applied.

Mk V ER672 at a wet Castle Bromwich in October 1942 and showing off the Vokes filter in detail.

Top: Mk VB EP455 of 601 Squadron between sorties.

Above: Mk VC BR202 with the Merlin 45 engine, revised nose and cowling contours and large long-range tank fitted, June 1943.

Right: Mk VB EN821 of 243 Squadron displays the cannon-type wing and depicts the unique planform with wing-fillet arcing back into the fuselage.

Servicing the Spitfire. Ground crew attend to an airframe. Note the panel in hood.

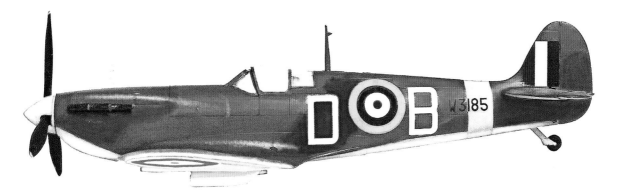

Spitfire Mk VA W3185, Tangmere Wing, Douglas Bader, 1941.

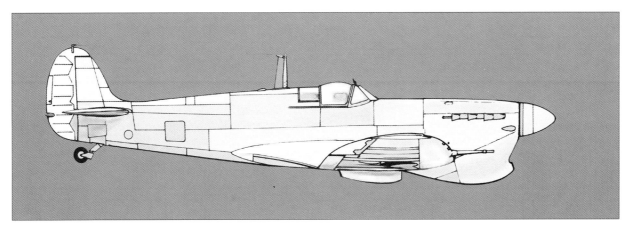

Line drawing of a Spitfire MKVB (Tropical).

# Variations on a Theme

From the Mk V and its airframe developments and from the ever-increasing Merlin power offering, Spitfire proved it could be developed from its 1934 design origins to a 1944 highlight that was a faster, heavier, more versatile aircraft, yet one which preserved its vital ingredients. Tailfins and wingtips might have been adapted, but the primary ingredients of the main wing design, fuselage, and Merlin powerplant, remained the core design elements of this

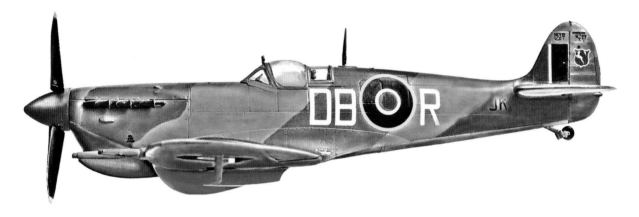

Spitfire MK VC, No. 2 Squadron, 7 Wing, SAAF, Sicily, 1944.

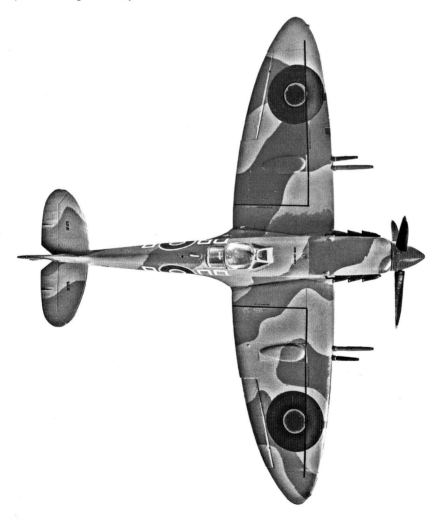

## Mk VI

From Mk V came the Mk VI as a dedicated high-altitude machine (40,00ft) that offered optional 'pointed' long-span (40ft 2in) elliptical wingtips specifically designed to perform in thinner air. A pressure cabin for the pilot (with externally mounted cabin air-feed pipe) also marked out this variant. The uprated Merlin 47 of 1,415hp/1056kW offered strong performance via a four-bladed propeller. Reinforced bulkheads in front of and behind the pilot created the pressurized cabin with a pressure differential of 2lbf/in$^2$ equating to giving 28,000ft at a true external height of over 40,000ft. Later Mk VIs had the pointed tailfin for greater directional control with high-power, thin-air combinations. Entering service in April 1942, 97 Mk VIs were manufactured: the first Mk VI was a converted Mk I as XV4942.

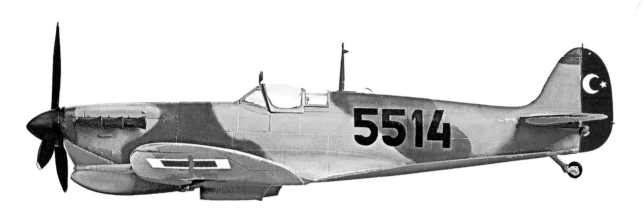

Spitfire VB (Trop), 1st Company, 5th Air Regiment, Bursa, Turkish Air Force, 1944.

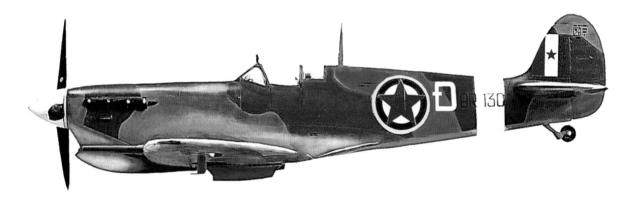

Spitfire Mk VC, 352 Squadron, Yugoslavia, 1944.

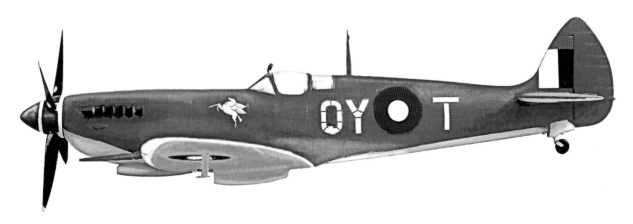

Spitfire VIII, 452 Squadron, Royal Australian Air Force, Northern Territory, 1944

### Mk VII

The Type 551 Mk VII was a deeper redesign of the Mk VI and used the two-stage supercharged Merlin 60 series (1,710hp/1276kW) for higher altitude work. Extra cooling was required and a new port side under wing air inlet fitted. All Mk VIIs featured the taller, pointed fin/rudder combination. Some featured a double-glazed canopy. A retractable tailwheel was a notable production item. To be noted were the revised chord ailerons. Maximum straight-line level speed was a stunning 408mph, but weight now aped the Hurricane's at 7,875lb, but in a far more potent machine. 145 Mk VIIs were manufactured in 1942–43 with Middle East theatre service from 1942.

### Mk VIII

From Mk VII stemmed the similar but unpressurized high-speed general-purpose Mk VIII which entered service in the Mediterranean theatre in August 1943. Whereas Mk V and its derivatives (including Mk IX) were airframes with a variety of add-ons for varying requirements, Mk VIII was a more defined collation of the known range of improvements all fitted to one variant under a new Mark on a new production line.

The three main models were L.F., F, or H.F., as low-, medium- or high-altitude variants: F.VIII with Merlin 61 or 63, H.F. VIII with the Merlin 70 and L.F.VIII with a Merlin 66 tuned for lower altitude efficiency. Some were fitted with tropical filters on the front chin. Many examples used the extended span Universal wing and later models adopted the revised taller fin and rudder. The F. Mk VIII operated in Italy and briefly in Russia (No. 155 Squadron) and in a fighter-bomber role. The first cut-down rear fuselage spine and teardrop canopy appeared on a Mk VIII. 1,658 Mk VIIIs were manufactured, nearly all serving overseas.

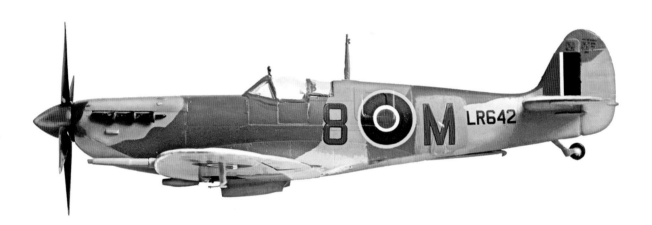

Seafire L IIC, 807 Naval Air Squadron, HMS *Battler*, 1943.

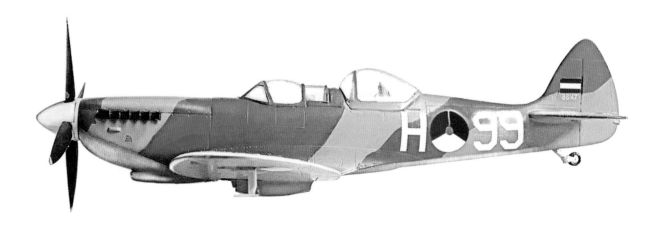

Mk IX trainer, Royal Netherlands Air Force JACTFS, Twente, 1948.

MK LF.IXE 26 GIAP PVO Leningrad USSR  1944-1945

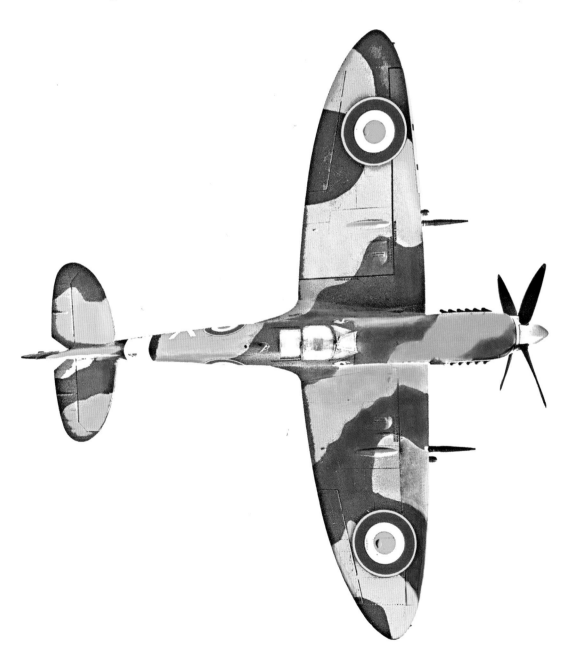

MKIX of the Armee de L'Air 1946

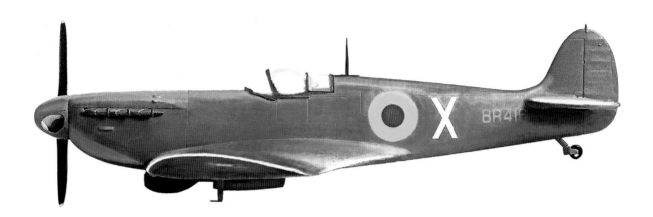

Spitfire PR1D BR416, No. 74 OTU, Palestine, 1944.

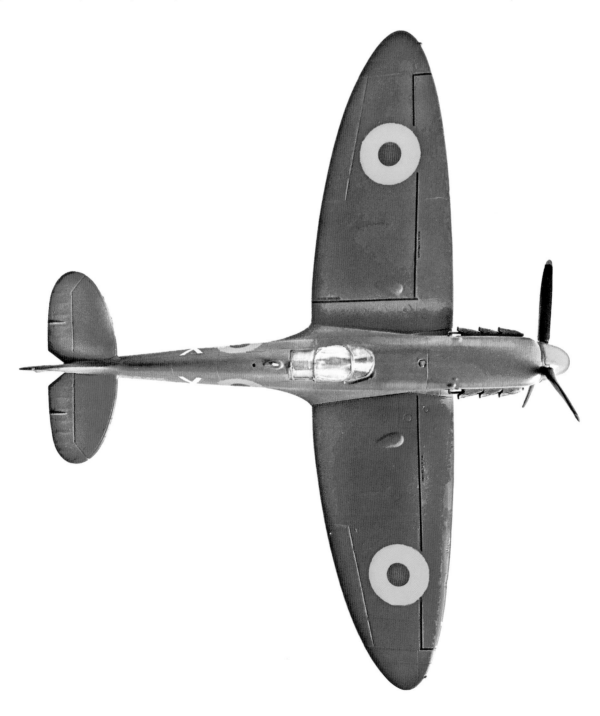

## Mk IX

As the Bf 109 was further developed and as the Luftwaffe was resurgent over Germany and France in 1942, a faster Mk V was urgently required to match the fast Bf 109 and even faster Fw 190 series. The answer was the Mk IX as a re-engined Mk V of June 1942 which saw production-line Mk Vs fitted with upgraded specifications to create the Mk IX. This saw the Merlin 60 series (1,475hp/1,100kW) and as Merlin 61 (1,565hp/1,167kW) in a lighter, revised Mk VC airframe. So was born Type 361, the Mk IX. A two-stage supercharger and two-speed, four-bladed Rotol propeller were applied. Low height power and high speed were required. Again, an L.F., F., or H.F., variant was offered that was dependent on engine type and tune. A larger forward fuel tank of 95 gallons, a rear fuselage 72-gallon tank and two 18-gallon wing fuel bags and an optional 50-gallon drop-tank were fitted: ultimate capacity of 253 gallons.

First deliveries were to No. 64 Squadron in July 1942. Latterly, in 1944, the Mk IX had its Universal C-type wing supplanted by a revised E-type wing. American M10 three-tube cluster launchers for 4.5in rockets were trialled in a Mk IX. By 1947, Mk IXs of the French Air Force would serve in French Indo-China based in Hanoi. The Royal Dutch Airforce would use Mk IXs in Java. By 1948, Mk IXEs of No. 332 Squadron Royal Norwegian Airforce took the Spitfire to colder climates.

A later variant with bubble canopy, taller tailfin/rudder resembled the Mk VI. Mk IX later switched to a ground-strafing role (but then needed and received clipped wings at 32ft 7in span) carrying a 500lb fuselage-mounted bomb and two 250lb bombs under the wings.

The taller fin and rudder and a rear-fuselage-mounted internal 72-gallon fuel tank created a strong package of which 5,665 were manufactured. Conversions included the tactical-reconnaissance F.R. IX., the P.R. IX and the basis for the two-seater trainer Tr. 9.

## L.F. XVI

This was the U.S. Packard-built Merlin 266, an engine that was not interchangeable with standard Merlin fitment or mounting. The airframe was similar to the Mk IX and offered with the Universal C wing but also optionable with the clipped wings for low-level work. Further modifications included the E wing and taller fin.

Mk VC AB320 in a classic tropical specification repose.

Mk VC AB320 shows off its later wing and classic modified ellipse wing planform in flight.

Mk LFV clipped-wing variant of 316 (Polish) Squadron.

Mk VB clipped wings and external tank.

### Mk XII & Sub-variants

This sub-variant was based on the Mk VC airframe (enlarged tailfin) but with a Griffon II engine (single stage supercharger), stronger fuselage, clipped wings and an optional retractable tailwheel. Max level flight speed was 398mph/640kph. Delivered to Nos 41 and 92 squadrons in February 1944, 100 were built. Of note it was from this airframe that the two-stage supercharger Griffon 61 series **Mk 21** (Type 356) derived. This featured extended-span wing changes; four 20-mm cannon were fitted and the undercarriage extended resulting in a track width increase. The **Mk XIV** (Type 372) derived from the work carried out to create the Mk 21. Six **Mk VIII** airframes were used as development types. The Griffon 65 and a five-bladed propeller, being noteworthy. Longer fuselages, taller fin, 'E' wing, and teardrop canopy featured as the airframes were developed. This high speed Spitfire was capable of tackling the Me 262 jet fighter over Germany in late 1944. It also out-performed the Bf 109G across most operating regimes. No. 610 Squadron was the launch unit. One Mk XIV was fitted with a contra-rotating propeller. 1,055, Mk XIV were manufactured. From Mk XIV came the larger, stronger, **Mk XVIII.** From **Mk 21**, Roman numeral nomenclature was dropped.

LF Mk VB NK-H of 118 Squadron.

62. PRVII X4786 displays the unarmed 'clean' wing and Merlin 45 powerplant.

### Photo-Reconnaissance (PR)

Although photo-reconnaissance Spitfires had been developed from the Mk II as PR types A–D, the Mk V then provided the basis for conversions to PR type as the PR Mk IV with larger fuel tanks with wing- and fuselage-mounted cameras. The confusing temporary designation of PR Mk V applied to the converted types of which 15 were fitted with Merlin 45 and Type C camera installations. Some had large wing tanks and other extra equipment including a teardrop high-visibility canopy without armoured glass The PR Mk VII had two vertically configured fuselage cameras (as opposed to wing-mounted cameras), and extra tankage in the body and armour.

Mk VC BR202 with long-range tank.

The clipped wings on AA 937 allow sight of the very smooth skinning to the forward fuselage.

Above: The Mk V-derived float plane with Supermarine floats designed by Arthur Shirvall.

Left and below: The high-altitude wingtips fitted to Mk VI X4942 aided the lift coefficient in thinner air.

The Spitfire wing root fairing design, armament blisters and modified Griffon engine cowling can be appreciated in this view.

### Seafire

Early 'Hooked Spitfires' as Seafires **Mk I** (Type 340) and **Mk IIC** (Type 351) were known were based on the Mk VC. The later, folding-wing Seafire **Mk III** (Type 358) derived from a separate design process yet had its origins in the converted Mk VC concept.

Adding a rear fuselage Vee-framed strengthening plate, arrestor hook, tie-down points, created the Seafire 1. A reinforced undercarriage and other modifications such as catapult reels and a hook created the Seafire **Mk IB** and **Mk IIC** – a Mk VC sub-variant. The initial modified Mk I numbered 48 airframes transferred to 802 Squadron of the Royal Navy in late 1941, with a further 119 airframes following of the revised model. Flight tested on ground 'deck' marked runways and the deck of HMS *Illustrious*, this Mk VB derivative was fitted with the arrestor hook. They became the first true Seafire sub-variant and given high-frequency naval radio equipment. No wing-folding was fitted to these early Seafires that were then based on HMS *Furious* – to be superseded by the later Seafires **Mks IIC**, **LIIC**, **LRIIC** and wing-folding **Mk III**, **FXV**, then to the Spitfire **Mk 21** series sub-variant as post-war Seafires **45**, **46**, **47** with Merlin and then Griffon engines.

Mk XII with more brutish lines than the original design. Note nose contours.

Overall, 22,750 Spitfire airframes were manufactured (including Seafires). It must surely be realized that Supermarine Spitfire was something far more than a 1930s' design, a national icon or a subject of wartime propaganda over its Hurricane compatriot. Spitfire contained aerodynamic science so advanced that its reality and how it was achieved, was deliberately obscured at the time and for decades afterwards. With the passing of years and in a new century, the full story of the Spitfire design, its designers – as well its pilots and combat history – can now be realized for the history-changing landmark that it was. Modern technology, computer-aided fluid dynamics, digital authority, all obscure what Supermarine achieved in shaping and building by hand and by calculus what was a massive advance that played a leading part in world history. Spitfire's development into MK V and its sub-variants, surely proved its genius and that of R. J. Mitchell and his team.

F Mk XVI SX336 (G-KASX) Griffon-powered double-folding wing Seafire displays its belly and arrestor hook details.

This close-up 1944-built Mk LFIXc (as UF-Q) was originally of the RCAF Hornet 433 Squadron and flown in combat in France. It shows the late-model wing blisters, revised engine cowling, and the important wing fillet sculpting. Seen in RAF 601 Squadron paint scheme (Balkans) as MJ250 of F/L D. Ibbotson.

Right and bottom: Ultra-smooth skinning and wing blister details captured in fully restored glory. Note the Spitfire's gull-wing setting to wing-to-fuselage design.

Mk VII MFD124 shows off the pointed wingtips and tailfin developments.

French Seafire XV 54.5-S of the Flotille 54S Aircraft Carrier *Arromanches*, Hyeres 1953–1954

# Modellers' Wings

Mk HF IXE 5503 of SAAF Air Operations School, AFS Laangebaan Weg, March 1951. Kit by ICM modelled by Frank Reynolds.

S pitfire has also become a modeller's icon, a favourite to which thousands of hours can be devoted. Dedicated Spitfire model makers take forensic

pride in checking the dimensions and configurations of any new Spitfire model and any errors or issues are likely to be quickly seized upon and discussed. The internet now provides the hobbyist or modeller with quick access to details and debate about models, specifications, schemes, and the nuances of build quality and, hybridization for the advanced forensic modeller. Hyperscale, Modelling Madness, Scale Mates, Modell Verisum, Cybermodeller, International Plastic Modellers Society (IPMS), all provide serious forums for debate and learning. Thankfully, the printed, essential, modelling magazines survive to continue their tradition of scale aircraft modelling excellence.

Arguably, the true beginning of the plastic modelling of the Spitfire started when the first **Airfix** aircraft kit was released in 1953 (or 1955 depending on claim) in the form of the Spitfire Mk I. The role of the Airfix 1:24 Mk IA as early as 1970 was defining in Spitfire modelling history and in Airfix's own story. The accuracy of detail, moulding representation, set a new standard. It was some time before Airfix and other kit makers tooled up for later Spitfire variants and learned from their experiences. In this period, modellers took to creating modified, hybrid versions of the Airfix Mk IA to represent later Marks, and continue to do so today.

Mk VB BM526 of VCS-7 US Navy, Lee-on-Solent, June 1944. Kit by Airfix modelled by Frank Reynolds.

Mk VB BM526 shows off the correct moulding and construction of the vital semi-elliptical wing, wing fillet and fuselage contours. Note the strengthening strips shown on each wing – a feature not common to all Mk Vs. The expert modeller will remove them if they are inappropriate to the variant being constructed.

As an example of how far we have come, Airfix issued in 2000 the Royal Air Force Battle of Britain Memorial (BBMF) Flight Supermarine Spitfire Mk VB. From 2011 to 2015, Airfix issued several new toolings for various further Spitfire Marks including both the Spitfire XII and Seafire XVII. A comparison of the two kits shows that each has been *separately* tooled and the parts frames are markedly different kit to kit, but thanks to CAD tooling, many parts are interchangeable from one kit to the other. The result is that modelling a Seafire XV is a realistic proposition.

Airfix launched models in several scales and of note, their Mk V kit was one of the first to accurately render the gullwing, underwing joint and concave U-channel detailing; many rivals did not. The recent Airfix (Hornby) mouldings are deemed to represent high-quality and accurate renditions of the Spitfire's essential details – wings, panels, rivets, hatches, cowlings and undercarriage.

Scales from 1:37, 1:44, 1:48, 1:72, 1:100, have proved popular as the lead sizes across the kit manufacturers. Of interest, one of the earliest Mk V kits was made by Marusan as a Mk VB at 1:100; released in 1963, it was re-boxed in 1967.

**Hasegawa** was a later arrival to the field of 1:48 scale aircraft, and its efforts may be seen as a response to Tamiya's brand-building. Hasegawa's early toolings stem from as far back as the 1980s and are regarded as leading exemplars of moulding and detail; however an issue with a too-short fuselage moulding in Hasegawa's Mk IX cannot go unmentioned. For some reason this tooling represented an inaccurate rear fuselage boom length that threw out the perspective of the aircraft and its design.

**Tamiya**, makers of highly detailed 'model' cars turned to the Spitfire early on and produced noteworthy results, including the Mk VB and Mk VB (Trop). Tamiya has made a major selling point of its accuracy, modelling quality and, of the fact that its Spitfire cowling panels (0.04mm thick) can be made detachable. Tamiya's ailerons have metal rod fixings, Like Airfix, the Tamiya Spitfire was spot on with the cockpit, gullwing, wing fillet and underwing U-channels – the vital details. But even the likes of Tamiya have been known to compromise in details such as undercarriage changes between Mk VC and the Mk IX when scissor-link undercarriage and wheel-well changes between the types altered such details. Exquisite and expensive, especially in larger scale, Tamiya's Spitfires, like its other models, reflect an art honed at its Shizouka base, where Tamiya has created a hardcore modelling culture.

As the modelling hobby developed apace into the 1980s and 1990s, manufacturers came to the Spitfire and other Marks became available. A range of lesser names such as Nichimo, Novo, Aurora, and then the Frog range (branded as Tri-Ang in France) proved popular up to its demise in 1976, but today, the names of Airfix, Tamiya, Revell, Hasegawa, Heller, ICM, Italeri, Pavla, Fujimi, Eduard, Monogram, Hobbyboss, Occidental, Trumpeter, Brigade, Minicraft

and Special Hobby, frame the modeller's renditions of the Spitfire.

Other kits have come from manufacturers such as Lotina, Lindberg, Pacific Coast, and Hawk/Testro. Rare 1:72 and 1:100 scale kits were produced by Nitto, and Maruson. The recent 1:32 scale fashion has seen Hobbyboss produce a Mk VB; previously only the 1980s' Hasegawa Mk V was available at this scale. Hobbycraft have issued a Mk VC at 1:24 based on a reissued Trumpeter kit. From 1997 Minicraft models made a Mk V which is a reissue of the earlier kit from Academy, itself taken from Crown's original 1973 tooling. Revell issued a Mk I in 1973 and Nichimo issued a 1:100 Mk II in 1969.

Mk IXE of the 26 GIAP PVO, Leningrad, USSSR 1944-1945. Hasegawa kit

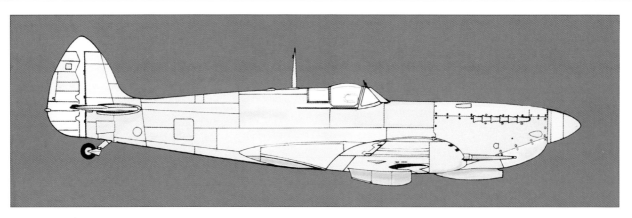

A line drawing of a Spitfire MKIX.

**Typical Mk V Kits**

Academy 1:144 Mk V WWII 50 Anniversary Collection (kit 4412) released 1993

Airfix 1:24 Royal Air Force BBMF Mk VB (kit A50055A) released 2000 from 1970 tooling

Airfix 1:24 Mk VB (kit A12005A) released 2013, re-tooled from 1973 original

Hasegawa 1:32 Mk VB (kit 08082) released 1994 original tooling 1987, 2017 revisions to parts

Hasegawa 1:32 Spitfire Mk VB Night Fighter (kit 08132) released 2002

Hasegawa 1:32 Mk V Clipped wings (kit S18 and ST2) released 1992

Hasegawa 1:32 Mk VI HF (pointed wingtips) (kit S16) released

Hobbyboss 1:32 Mk VB (kit 83205) released 2011 new tooling

Hobbycraft 1:24 Mk VC (kit HC1802) reissued Trumpeter tooling

Revell 1:32 U.S. Army Spitfire MK5C (kit H281) released in 1975, re-tooled in 2014

Tamiya 1:48 Mk V and MK VB (Trop)
Tamiya 1:72 Mk VB (kit 60756)

Trumpeter 1.24 Mk VB (kit 02043) released 2003

Trumpeter 1:24 Mk Vb / Trop (kit 02412) released 2003 with later modifications

Trumpeter 1:24 Mk Vb Floatplane (kit 02404) released 2004

Hybrid kits constructed from various components provide a rich seam for modelling expression. The Pavla range of modifications of Spitfire parts ranging from wingtips to seats, fuel tanks etc. allow the modeller to individualize their chosen kit. An extensive range of decals on the accessory market also allow 'customization' of scale airframes.

Shared mouldings are not unusual with sub-licensing deals in the kit world. For example, Revell's later mouldings seem to stem from the Ukrainian ICM Spitfire series, which have been around for two decades. The issue with such tooling as brand-engineering is that some parts can show signs of mould wear – requiring work from the modeller. Such issues were obvious in 1970s' Soviet product mouldings.

Occasionally, errors creep in but are often quickly rectified, e.g. Occidental's Mk IX had a problem with the shape of its nose and cowling top. ICM's Spitfire early kits suffered from some moulding and excess flash issues.

As we know, building Spitfire's advanced technology presented the Supermarine prototype builders with challenges, but reaped massive rewards for the Spitfire in its battle-winning advantage. Today's modeller faces similar Spitfire wing-building challenges, especially the flying-model builder who cannot use the original full-size Spitfire aerofoils at model scale and must therefore experiment.

Both colour photographs on page 48 and above: Mk VC of No. 2 Squadron, 7 Wing, SAAF, Sicily (Vokes filter, long-range tank and cannon wing.) Tamiya/Special hobby kit.

Mk IXE 664L, Royal Egyptian Air Force, 1948. Kit by Hasegawa.

Top and above: These views show Seafire IIIs from 807 Squadron RNAS of HMS *Hunter*, Fleet Air Arm, British East Indies Fleet, Andaman Sea, May 1945. Note fuselage reinforcement mouldings. Kit by Special Hobby modelled by Frank Reynolds.

Seafire L. III 894 RNAS of HMS *Indefatigable*, Sakashima Gunto, May 1945, British Pacific Fleet. Pilot: Sub-Lieutenant Richard Reynolds.

## Detail Delight

There are many exquisite and forensic details that the modeller can apply to his or her specific interpretation of a Spitfire whatever its Mark.

Typical points of discussion include: Should the cockpit seat detailing be depicted of the steel of Bakelite type? Should the ailerons of a fabric-skinned aileron variant feature the 6–10-inch balancing strips of cord material that were glued to the ailerons' trailing edge? Should a metal-skinned aileron depiction allow for the small deflections on the metal that were used to trim the aileron's balance? Is it really possible to depict elevator trim tabs at small scale? Are the flaps static or moveable? Are the wing armament cannon 'blister' bulges correctly shaped and accurately moulded?

What of the underwing and fuselage belly design details and their moulding quality in a kit? Are the scooped-out concave, inverted U-channels that feature under each wing root and run backwards to the fuselage boom, correctly moulded to the required depth and shape or is handiwork needed? Prior to the current 1:44 and 1:72 Spitfires across several manufacturers that have *finally* addressed this issue, many early kits did not. Airfix was an early exemplar of meeting this challenge.

There are many issues of discussion: Are the radiators and intakes correct in shape and detail? Many are not. Is the dihedral angle correct? Is the wing fillet appropriately moulded? What of the fuselage rivets, hatch details, plate lines and engine cover mouldings? Is the tropical filter correct? Are the guns or cannons correctly detailed? The canopy and windscreen? The undercarriage? What of the pilot's rear-view mirror – should it be rectangular or round?

Is your paint colour really accurate? How old is the pigment? Have you really researched the correct colours, say, for example, an engine oil pipe or a cooling hose? Can you accurately match ageing effects on alloy, copper and rubber? Are you using the correct hue for the exhaust or the cockpit interior sidewall? Is your cockpit interior sidewall the correct shape or a reverse side to an external moulding? Is the pilot wearing the correct uniform and life jacket? Painting the MK V in desert camouflage needs care with shades. Sun bleaching occurred quickly. Wet season mud spray on the airframe can be considered: Dark Earth and Middle Stone above with Azure Blue underneath need careful portrayal depending on the theatre chosen.

What of worn finishes depicting in-service aircraft? Experts advise the modeller to be careful not to overdo scuff and scratch rendition, nor to allow too much 'alloy' showing through. If depicting a model prior to combat, remember to cover over the gun ports (using roundel red transfer cut-outs). Depicting combat repairs and replacement panels also adds realism.

The fitting of a highly detailed Merlin and engine bay is a favourite for the dedicated modeller; an electric motor to power the propeller can also add to the display.

All these and many more are the nuances of modelling the Spitfire. If you want to get forensic, this is the route to achieving it.

The well-known trap for less-experienced Spitfire modellers lies in defining the variations that exist in armament, the variations of wingtips, fins, rudders, engine cowlings and fuselage configurations.

Perhaps the key thing to consider when modelling the aircraft is what the modeller wants to achieve and to then focus upon as much information as possible to create a defined speciality. Key steps must include preparing the kits parts prior to construction. Cleaning the parts (while still on the sprue?), trimming and generally fettling prior to offering up for construction, can pay many dividends. As with painting a full-size aircraft or a car, preparation is key

American Spitfires Mk VB (Trop) of 4FS, 52FG, USSAF and Mk VB of US Navy VCS-7, 1944.

Mk IX 101, Squadron, Israeli Air Force,1949. Hasegawa kit,

Mk IX trainer, Royal Netherlands Air Force JACTFS, Twente, 1948; one of three delivered. Kit by Hasegawa /Brigade Models.

to the final result. Remember, it is vital to paint many parts prior to assembly. This particularly applies to the cockpit interior and fittings, the engine, its bay, and inside any wells or inspection hatches that open. And what about self-mixing of paint to achieve a more accurate rendition? Why not.

When modelling a Spitfire, and specifically the Mk V, good reference sources are essential to get the right combination of features. Any risk of guesswork can be lessened by focusing on an exact airframe and securing as many visual references for it as possible – hence the 'inspired' guesstimate.

Top modellers are happy to reshape a moulding using modelling filler, but experience is necessary before you attack the mouldings. This is where referring to photographs of the actual Spitfire you are attempting to depict in scale becomes vital. Otherwise, shapes, radii, skin and scaling can all go wrong.

Accuracy may be 'king' but the modeller might be unwise to conform to perceived wisdoms as rules. This is particularly

true when modelling the Mk V and all its sub-variants, not least because the Mk V and its offspring were subject to so many modifications not just at the factory, but also in-theatre, in the field of battle across the world – where local squadron engineers, mechanics and fitters could and did apply their personal tweaks and changes to their airframes. So who is to say what is correct or incorrect? Following actual manuals, drawings, spec sheets and notably, photographic evidence, must be the best technique and one better to be defended. So why not choose a specific aircraft as identified and create a model from actual in-service photographs of it?

The Hasegawa Mk V has been manufactured for two decades and, in the opinion of many, set the standard in its detailing and options alongside recent Airfix offerings. From the baseline Hasegawa kit, you can construct a full-span or clipped wing version of the Mk VB. Of note, the option exists to create a fuselage with standard nose contours and intake, or a Mk VB with the full-chested Vokes (tropical) air filter, or the smaller frontal area Aboukir version. Numerous propeller and spinner options can be tried. Vitally, the external or internal windscreen armour can be optioned – with different windscreens being provided.

Mk VIII A58-435 of 452 Squadron Royal Australian Air Force, Northern Territory, 1944. Kit by Hasegawa.

Normal and clipped-wing variants: Mk VA Douglas Bader, Tangmere Wing, 1941, and Mk XII, No. 41 Squadron, Tangmere, 1943. Both by Airfix.

External detail satisfaction is achieved via a combination of recessed seams and raised panel lines, fabric rudder detail and the 'proper' metal-covered ailerons found on Mk Vs. Details such as the retract-extend indicator rods on the wings are present albeit moulded. So too are the special undercarriage locking lugs. The cockpit is a highlight notably with the correct internal contours to the side walls. A highly detailed seat with all the correct items adds to the lustre. Detailing is a key element of the kit, noteworthy being the open-frame rear bulkhead, seat frame details, well moulded levers, and an engraved-style instrument panel. Some modellers feel the only real issue is the scaling of the pilot's control column.

The flaps are only hinted at and some minor works with putty/filler and filing is appropriate for the experienced modeller who wishes to modify the wing. Is this kit the defining early opportunity for the non-forensic expert modeller to build a Mk V without too much corrective fettling or experience required?

Hasegawa issued its own variation of the Mk V's when it launched its HF Mk VI as a version of the high-altitude fighters built to address the Luftwaffe Ju 86 high-altitude photo-recce airframe.

Mk IXE 26 GIAP. The Leningrad Spitfire, 1944–45. Hasegawa.

Mk VB (Trop), 'Major Levine', 4FS, 52FG, USAAF, June 1943. Airfix.

# Model Showcase

## Mission to Model
## Frank Reynolds's Spitfire Passion

Frank Reynolds is the modeller with a forensic eye for detail and modification who has constructed 56 Spitfire models in tribute to the aircraft and whose work appears online worldwide, and herein. Here, Frank offers the reader an example of modelling expertise and enthusiasm in a commentary about a version of the Mk V he built:

'War weary but refurbished Mk Vs were found in the inventory of the South African Air Force, Turkey and Yugoslavia, all of whom had influence in the Mediterranean Theatre of the Second World War. It is the air force of Turkey that provides the interest for one of my projects, an air force that has the intriguing claim to fame of being the only one to simultaneously operate the Spitfire and Focke Wulf Fw 190 in its fighter squadrons! A neutral country during the war, Turkey was able to accept deliveries of war material from both sides of the conflict.

'Turkey initially accepted three Mk I Spitfires in late 1939, but further deliveries were delayed until 1944, after some years of negotiations to persuade Turkey to cut off trade and diplomatic relations with the Axis Powers. A total of 105 aircraft were supplied, some 36 Mk VBs and 69 Mk VCs. Drawn from RAF Middle East stocks, they were used primarily for training by the 5th and 6th air regiments. The VBs were withdrawn in 1948 and the VCs a year later.

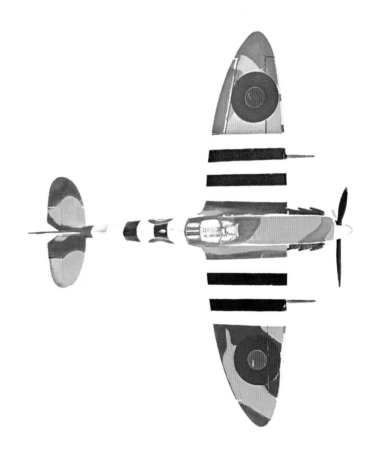

Mk VB BM526 of VCS-7, US Navy, Lee-on-Solent, June 1944.

Mk VB BM526 of VCS-7, US Navy, Lee-on-Solent, June 1944.

Design detail: note accurate rendition of cowling, exhaust and fuselage skin variations.

Detail of rudder area extension as seen on French Seafire of the Flotille 54.S.

Mk XV hybrid, No. 1 Squadron, Union of Burma Air Force, 1953. Airfix hybrid kit.

Mk VC, 352 Squadron, Yugoslavia, 1944. Kit by Special Hobby.

Seafire XVII SP343 of the 1832 Naval Air Squadron RNVR Southern Air Division, Culham 1950 with double folding wing. Airfix Kit

Seafire XVII and Seafire 47 wing folding mechanism comparison

'When modelling a Spitfire V, good reference sources are essential to get the right combination of features and it will always be a trap for the unwary. Sometimes the only answer is the inspired guess – but one guided by vital visual and data reference source materials.

'This new tooling is supplied in Airfix's now standard top-opening box. The parts are very cleanly moulded with no evidence of flash or sinkage and are beautifully engraved with sharp, clean panel lines and subtle fabric texture to the rudder and elevators. The transparent parts are reasonably well done but there is some distortion visible in the cockpit hood mouldings.

'Instructions consist of a 14-page booklet with construction steps set out in 46 pictorial stages keyed to CAD drawings with the relevant parts colour-coded to each stage

'This project represents the 'other version' offered by Airfix – a Mk VB/Trop incorporating the massive chin air intake/filter, the later type windscreen with more bulged cockpit hood and the large Rotol propeller.

'Construction begins with the interior, which features separate cockpit side walls which also form the interior of the lower fuselage. There are four bulkheads providing the engine firewall, instrument panel, pilot's seat support and headrest support. The seat is well detailed with separate sides, rear armour plate, seat frame and head rest. Well detailed levers, pedals, trim wheels and oxygen bottle are separately moulded. The cockpit interior was finished in Xtracrylix XA1010 Interior Grey Green, with the section aft of the seat in Tamiya XF-16 Flat Aluminium. The instrument panel, control boxes and handles were picked out in Flat Black. The kit provides an effective decal for the instrument faces and seat belts were fashioned from painted masking tape.

'The entire cockpit pod is trapped between the fuselage halves and it is a very tight fit, needing a degree of juggling and fettling to get it right. This is a stage of construction that demands care and a good deal of test/dry-fitting the sub assemblies. The kit provides alternative windscreens and canopies to cover the different variants on offer and to accommodate the whole upper cowling between the engine and cockpit is a separate U-shaped component. This was a reasonable fit but the tops of the bulkheads needed some trimming before the top cover would sit down satisfactorily. Before the fuselage halves are joined a decision has to be made as to whether the cockpit hood is to be open or closed. If closed, an appropriate transparency is provided, but the upper edges of the cockpit have to be trimmed away about 1mm to a scribed line moulded into the fuselage halves.

'The lower wing is a full span section and in a departure from Airfix tradition, the flaps are moulded in place – with no option for deployed flaps. The walls to the circular wheel wells are glued to the lower surface. The wing is provided with front and rear stub spars that span between the wheel wells and help to set up the vital, correct dihedral. An unusual undercarriage arrangement has been tooled, whereby each leg has an angled pintle (stub) at the top of the leg that fits into the rear face of the front spar, the remainder of the gear leg is to be added later. The spars and leg stub/pivot were found to be a very close fit and some shaving and fettling of the parts was necessary. I chose to add the lower wing section to the underside of the fuselage and then add the separate left and right upper wing mouldings. The upper wing panels incorporate the elliptical tips. Airfix have moulded two prominent strengthening strips on the upper surface of each wing, a feature that is not found on all Mk VBs.

Mk VB (Trop) 5514, 1st Company 5th Air Regiment, Bursa, Turkey, 1944. Kit by Airfix modelled by Frank Reynolds.

'Having established that they were not applicable to the Turkish machine being modelled, I carefully carved the strips away, using a fresh scalpel blade. The ailerons are separate and very finely cast. There is minimal joining area between the ailerons and the wing cut-out so they are vulnerable to breakage and I had to re-glue each one after some careless handling during construction.

The horizontal tails consist of separate upper and lower surfaces that fit positively into sockets in the fuselage. The elevators are a one-piece component with a central joining bar. I find it easier to cut the two elevator sections apart and to line them up when gluing either side of the tailfin. The one-piece rudder can now be added and the various flying surfaces checked for alignment.

The lower section of the engine cowl needed some adjustment to get it to seat into the leading edge of the wing. The underwing radiator and oil cooler show the degree of sophistication that is found in current Airfix kits with moulded fine mesh detail inside the components and a positionable outlet door on the radiator housing. These parts fit snugly into positive recesses in the lower wings.

The canopy was added and I chose the closed option, not forgetting to add the gun sight before the canopy went on. The hood and fixed rear section are supplied in one piece, with a separate windscreen. They were secured with Airfix Clearfix glue, then masked with Tamiya tape trimmed with a fresh scalpel blade. Next I added the wing cannon.

The propeller assembly has a positive keying system to prevent the blades from being assembled backwards. The spinner was painted Sky in Xtracrylix XA1007, with the blades in Flat Black and tips picked out in Yellow. The prop assembly was set aside while painting was carried out.

The colour scheme was taken from Tigerhead Decals sheet 48008 *Spitfires and Wurgers of the Turkish Air Force*. These provide a selection of two FW 190A-3s, a Spitfire IX and two Spitfire VBs. The decals are well printed in good register and packed with a small header card that simply shows side views of three of the five colour schemes. Although I found the decals quite satisfactory, I disagreed with Tigerhead over the configuration of the camouflage pattern shown in their instructions. I chose the option to finish the aircraft as 5514 of the 1st Company, 5th Air Regiment based at Bursa and there is an excellent photograph for reference of that airframe in the *Spitfire International*. This shows a British 'B' pattern camouflage scheme, so I copied the overall pattern from the 4-view drawings supplied with Tamiya's 1:48 Spitfire Mk I

The basic airframe was finished overall in grey auto primer. Any small gaps and scratches could be touched in at this stage although the fit of parts is so good that only the smallest amount of filler was required.

The aircraft is finished in the standard RAF-style desert scheme of the era, the underside airbrushed in Xtracrylix XA1026 Azure Blue, the upper surfaces shadow shaded in Xtracrylix XA1009 Middle Stone and XA1002 Dark Earth. The upper colours were divided with sausages of Blu-tack to provide a slightly feathered camouflage demarcation line. The rudder was picked out in Tamiya XF-7 Flat Red over a white undercoat and the propeller assembly in XF-1 Flat Black. All of the paint was applied with an Iwata HP-C airbrush. The whole airframe was then brushed with Future/Klear floor polish to provide a good base for the decals.

The decals went on fairly easily assisted with Micro Sol and Micro Set. Tigerhead provide only the main national markings and codes but the photos that I have seen indicate that the Turkish Spitfires had little in the way of obvious stencilling. Wing walk lines came from the Airfix decal sheet and I added a few of their RAF-type stencils to the underside to break the monotony of the all-blue paintwork. The decals were sealed with an airbrushed coat of Xracrylix XFF Flat varnish.

The undercarriage is added next but Airfix's approach to the assembly is far from conventional and demands care. The join between the undercarriage legs and the pintle/stub arrangement housed in the wing is shallow and potentially weak. It is definitely not novice-model-maker-friendly. The main leg and in-wing stub each have a flat section cut onto them to serve as a half-lapped joint. At the same time the instructions show that each leg has to be angled forward by 77 degrees and set up at 93 degrees splay to the wing under-surface. I left the wheels off to avoid a dead weight on the end of the legs while I tacked then in place with tube cement and then pushed and prodded them for about half an hour while waiting for the cement to go off, constantly checking the legs alignment against the drawings in the instructions.

'' still wonder whether this clever arrangement is over-engineered. In about 60 years of plastic kit production most manufacturers seem to agree that the easy way to secure a single leg undercarriage is to have a peg on top of the leg and a socket in the wing. It is a reasonably strong system and virtually self-aligning. It is a system that Airfix use in their relatively recent 1:48 scale kits of Spitfire XII, Spitfire XIX and Seafire XVII. I prefer that traditional arrangement. Left overnight to dry the legs still looked fragile so I extended the upper edge of the gear doors with a sliver of 20 thou. plastic card. This enabled me to glue the doors to both the wing underside and the legs and stiffen up the structure. The wheels were added once I was satisfied that the undercarriage structure had well and truly set hard.

'The engine exhausts were attached, painted in Tamiya XF-64 Red Brown, overlaid with X-33 Bronze. Finally, adding the pitot head, mirrors and propeller assembly completed another enjoyable build.

'In spite of the issues with the undercarriage assembly I still rate this as a great kit. Teamed with the Tigerhead decals it makes an interesting and unusual subject and comparison with the standard Mk VB makes a contrast in configuration. The kit is comprehensive, and a lot of thought has gone into its design. It repays careful work but it is not a kit for a beginner. The only filler needed was the slightest trace along main joint lines. This kit is highly recommended'

Seafire LIII, No. 1 Squadron, Irish Air Corps. 1948. Kit by Special Hobby modelled by Frank Reynolds.

PR1D (Aboukir filter) of No. 74 OUT, Palestine, 1944. Tamiya kit.

Such a commentary and the photographs of the Reynolds model collection shown here, prove just what can be achieved with deep knowledge of the Spitfire's design and dedicated research into its operational history. As with the original Spitfire itself, the modelling of this icon is complex but rewarding, providing the enthusiast with massive scope for self-expression and for the opportunity to pay tribute to the men that made, and flew, the Supermarine Spitfire – the aircraft that advanced the art of aerodynamics and which changed the course of world history.

MkIXC ML214 of No. 126 Squadron RAF, in D-Day markings.

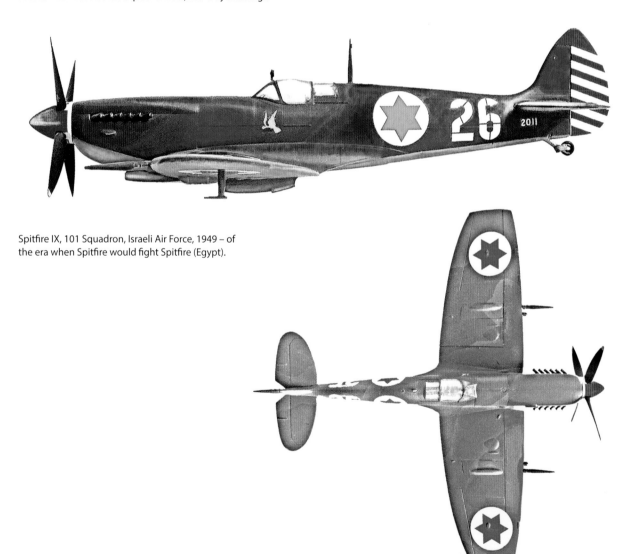

Spitfire IX, 101 Squadron, Israeli Air Force, 1949 – of the era when Spitfire would fight Spitfire (Egypt).

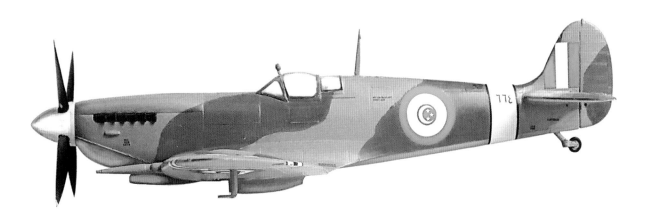

Mk IXE 664L, Royal Egyptian Air Force, 1948.

Seafire III, 807 Squadron RNAS of HMS *Hunter*, Fleet Air Arm, British East Indies Fleet, Andaman Sea, May 1945.

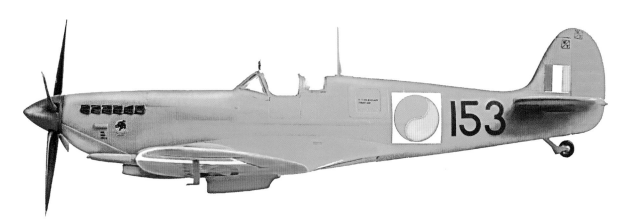

Seafire L III, No. 1 Squadron, Irish Air Corps. 1948.

Hellenic Spitfire. MK IXC MH508 of No 336 Squadron Greek Air Force, Sedes 1947. Hasegawa kit

MKIX NH520 Armee de L'Air Indo China 1946. Hasegawa kit

**Acknowledgements & Sources**

This book has been created from a number of sources including the author's title, *Secrets of the Spitfire: The Story of Beverley Shenstone, the Man who Perfected the Elliptical Wing* (Pen & Sword). This title was largely based upon the legacy and private papers of Beverley S. Shenstone, who worked for R. J. Mitchell. I am indebted to the modeller Frank Reynolds for his superb skills and Spitfire knowledge. The website modellingmadnees. com also provided reference points via Frank's contributions. Further sources include correspondence to, and from, B. S. Shenstone with leading figures, including Alfred Price, Roy Cross and the replies that so informed Mr Cross's subsequent book, with Gerald Scarborough, about the Spitfire, *Spitfire, Classic Aircraft No. 1: Their history and how to model them* (Patrick Stephens Ltd) as well as William Green's *Famous Fighters of the Second World War* (Doubleday). Other sources are J. A. D. Ackroyd's & P. J. Lamont's 'A comparison of turning radii for four battle of Britain fighter aircraft' (*The Aeronautical Journal* February 2000, pp. 53-58); J. A. D. Ackroyd's 'The Spitfire Wing Planform: A Suggestion' (*Journal of Aeronautical History* Paper No. 2013/02); *Spitfire in Action: Aircraft No. 39* by Jerry Scutts, illustrated by Don Greer and Rob Stern (Squadron/Signal Publications); *Spitfire 75*, edited by Ken Ellis *et al* (Key Publishing); communications with Mitchell's son, Dr G. Mitchell; communications with Dr Alfred Price and his *The Spitfire Story* (Weidenfeld Military); J. R Vensel's & W. H Phillips's 'Stalling Characteristics of Supermarine Spitfire VA Airplane' (National Advisory Committee for Aeronautics, September 1942 (declassified)); earlier discussions with Group Captain Sir Douglas Bader at Marlston, Berkshire. Photographs and illustrations: all illustrations, cover and modern-era photos are by the author or from his archive. Original-era photos are courtesy of the Phillip Jarrett Archive. Other Supermarine and Spitfire photos (1931–34) are courtesy of the B. Shenstone archive.